TIMELES
OF THE E
a beginr

RONALD L. BONEWITZ, PHD

Hodder & Stoughton
A MEMBER OF THE HODDER HEADLINE GROUP

To Reverend Paul Solomon
Founder of an interfaith church which saw the oneness of all

Acknowledgements

Many thanks are due to Guy and Meriel Ballard for their support, and to Lilian Verner-Bonds, as always.

Order queries: please contact Bookpoint Ltd, 39 Milton Park, Abingdon, Oxon OX14 4TD. Telephone: (44) 01235 400414, Fax: (44) 01235 400454. Lines are open from 9.00–6.00, Monday to Saturday, with a 24-hour message answering service.
Email address: orders@bookpoint.co.uk

British Library Cataloguing in Publication Data
A catalogue record for this title is available from The British Library

ISBN 0 340 70482 9

First published 1999
Impression number   10 9 8 7 6 5 4 3 2 1
Year   2003 2002 2001 2000 1999

Copyright © 1999 Ronald L. Bonewitz

All rights reserved. No part of this publication may be reproduced or transmitted in any form or by any means, electronic or mechanical, including photocopy, recording, or any information storage and retrieval system, without permission in writing from the publisher or under licence from the Copyright Licensing Agency Limited. Further details of such licences (for reprographic reproduction) may be obtained from the Copyright Licensing Agency Limited, of 90 Tottenham Court Road, London W1P 9HE.

Typeset by Transet Ltd, Coventry, England.
Printed in Great Britain for Hodder & Stoughton Educational,
a division of Hodder Headline Plc, 338 Euston Road, London NW1 3BH
by Cox & Wyman.

Contents

Introduction		1
	Guided visualizations	3
	How to do a meditation or visualization	5
Chapter 1	Setting the scene: everyday life in ancient Egypt	7
	Life in ancient Egypt	9
	Organization of Egyptian society	12
	Nubia	15
	Egyptian history	15
Chapter 2	The mystery begins: pyramids	19
	The mother mountain	20
	Inside the pyramid	21
	The symbolism of pyramids	23
	Visualization: The pyramid visualizations	25
Chapter 3	The 'Great God': Egyptian religion	28
	Gods, gods and more gods	29
	Strange gods?	30
	Degeneration of religious practice	32
	Early beliefs	35
	The ka, the ba and the ib	36
	The Weighing of the Heart	37
	Visualization: Experiencing the 'Great God'	38
Chapter 4	Gods and goddesses: mythology and the Goddess	40
	Mythology and religion	42
	Gods and goddesses	43
	The absent God	45
	The lost Goddess	47
	Exercise: Meeting the Goddess	48
Chapter 5	Isis and the Goddess principle	50
	The Isis and Osiris story	51
	Messages of the Isis–Osiris story	55
	The status of women in ancient Egypt	56
	Marriage	57
	Sexuality	58
	Women and sexuality in the New Kingdom	58
	Visualization: Finding the barriers to the natural you	59

Chapter 6	The rhythms of the Nile	62
	Rhythms connected to health and well-being	62
	The rhythms of time	65
	Earth rhythms	66
	Exercises	71
Chapter 7	Out of the fire: the hero's journey	73
	Visualization: Finding the hero inside yourself	78
Chapter 8	The return of the Goddess	80
	How we are separated from Goddess beliefs	81
	Re-establishing the Goddess principle	83
	Human social living	84
	Re-examining our beliefs	86
	The environment	87
	The Goddess and individuality	88
	Loosening the family tie	88
	Meditation	89
	References	90

Introduction

In a book about 'wisdom', the first question must be: 'What is wisdom?' Most of us have an instinctive feel for the answer, but putting it into words requires an effort. The dictionary tells us that wisdom has the qualities of common sense and intelligence. We also discover that wisdom involves prudence, insight, understanding and enlightenment. For each of these words we can find yet other words and eventually we can fill a page with them – without completely describing wisdom. Most of us recognize that there are qualities to wisdom that are beyond words. We all know them. We can all sense them. But there are really no words for them except – wisdom. But most of us would agree on one thing: there is a timeless, eternal quality to wisdom. Something which touches the most profound inner truths in each of us, no matter who we are or where we come from. It is this eternal dimension that we will seek in ancient Egyptian wisdom.

The most imposing problem in a book about Egyptian wisdom is the immense antiquity of Egyptian life. The Egypt we are concerned with came essentially to an end with the conquest of Egypt by the Hyskos in about 1780 BC, when Egyptian life and religion became infused with their influences; and it came finally and utterly to an end over 300 years before the birth of Christ, when Egypt was conquered by Alexander the Great and became a Greek province. The majority of surviving written material is after this date and is strongly influenced by Greek thinking: it is really no longer Egyptian at all. A classic example is The Hermetica, a series of writings in Greek, resembling the dialogues of Plato, but said to originate with the Egyptian god Thoth. The earliest eras of Egyptian life, those which interest us the most, are so far in the past that they are hard for us to grasp. During Cleopatra's reign more than 30 years before the birth of Christ, the pyramids were already 2,000 years old.

We must also be careful in deciding which aspects of Egyptian life have a relevancy today. The way we think about ourselves, others and the world around us are vastly different between then and now. If we were to ask, for example, 'How did the Egyptians *see* the role of women in their society?', implying they gave it thought, there can be no answer because no Egyptian would have ever asked the question. A woman's role was predetermined by her birth and no one would have even thought to question it. The relevant question is 'What *was* the role of women in Egyptian society?' We can describe what the role was with some accuracy, but without asking a question that requires the Egyptians to have thought about things the same way we do. It is an important distinction.

Equally, we must also be careful not to make judgements of Egyptian life based on modern life. It was, at the time, neither good nor bad, because other options simply weren't available – often because they had never even been thought of. Certainly, if such conditions existed today they would be utterly unacceptable, but only because we now have choices and know differently.

There are also limits on account of the Egyptian style of writing. The Egyptians, while possessing an excellent written language, saw writing itself in a way entirely different from today. In particular, if something was 'common knowledge', they saw no need to write it down. Thus some of the most important aspects of Egyptian life were those aspects which would have been, by their very nature, 'common knowledge'. There are references to them in other writings, but we can only infer them. Understanding their context goes a long way towards revealing them, however.

Each chapter of this book examines both Egyptian wisdom and its modern counterpart. To help gain an inner understanding of Egyptian wisdom, there is a brief visualization at the end, to help attune the reader in an experiential way to what the text reveals.

There are many books which purport to reveal secret Egyptian mysteries. This is not one of those, in that it does not rely on Greek interpretations of Egyptian wisdom. Within the everyday lives and beliefs of the ancient Egyptians millennia before the Greeks, there is no shortage of tangible wisdom, wisdom that can enrich and enhance and, perhaps, even help to preserve, our lives today. We are aided in this by one true fact – people are still people. The profound wisdom that enabled Egyptian civilization to survive for 3,000 years cannot help but be meaningful, reaching us as it does, across the ages.

Guided visualizations

Within this book are a number of guided visualizations, to aid the reader in connecting to that portion of him or herself that is one with the ancient wisdoms explored in this book. Some readers may have no experience either with visualization or meditation. For those readers, a brief word: meditation and visualization are simply a form of relaxation. The images that are suggested in each visualization are carefully chosen to stimulate that portion of one's being that identifies with the archetypal figures and situations described herein. As we will discover in this book, these are universal and part of everyone. Because they are universal, they touch on dimensions of our beingness that are often not accessed through life in the 'normal' world, the world where many of these wisdoms have been forgotten. The purpose of this book and of these visualizations is to reawaken that which has been forgotten, that which sustained and enriched the lives of not only the ancient Egyptians, but of peoples everywhere. In our 'modern' world we have lost touch with much of our deepest heritage as humans. It has been our great loss. The social problems and upheavals that surround us are in no small measure due to this. There are many ways to recover that which has been lost and what is offered here is but a small portion of what is available. But it is an incredibly rich source. Let us never forget – *it sustained Egypt for over 3,000 years.*

A word about past lives

Some readers may have already experienced, or will experience, memories of past lives. For those who have not, and for those for whom the idea of past lives is not acceptable, be assured that there is nothing in this text that requires such a belief. The archetypes we will uncover in our exploration of Egyptian wisdom are universal and timeless. Thus in the guided imagery that is part of this book, use the images as just that – prototype images that are as valid today as they were in ancient times.

For those readers who have experienced past-life memories, many will remember a life in Egypt. That is fairly likely, because, if we think of it, 3,000 years of human history happened in Egypt, so it would be surprising if we had not.

An understanding of past-lives does permit one important step forward in growth: as you become more and more aware of your own aspect of choice in coming into life, you will become increasingly aware that all that has happened to you in this life has been your creation and your choosing. Every person who has 'caused' you pain and suffering has been trying to teach you something and you attracted these people to you consciously or unconsciously for just that purpose. This idea will be further expanded as we progress.

Further, the fundamental point of past-life work is *not* about remembering past lives – it is about remembering the unfinished lessons of past lives. Life is about learning, whether in this life or others. There is a temptation to get hung-up on past lives, the 'I-was-so-and-so'. Forget it. What was the *lesson* of being so-and-so? The Egyptians put great store in the body as a vehicle for movement into what was beyond. They were correct. It is a *vehicle*.

There is another point to remember: many of us carry a deep guilt about wanting to be alive and wanting to have a body, as we believe that in doing so we have separated ourselves from the source of our own being. For many of us, perhaps for all of us, our experience of having our first body was as if we cut ourselves off from God in order to get it. Learning to live in the body and still be fully connected to the source of your being is ultimately the only lesson.

How to do a visualization or meditation

1 Create a sacred space

For the ancient Egyptians the whole world was a sacred place. But our lives have become so intense, practical and economic in their orientation that the claims of the moment are so great we hardly know where we are. So creating a personal, sacred space is an absolute necessity, whether you meditate in it or where you can simply experience and bring forth what you are and what you might be. It can be a room, or a certain hour or so in the day, or some music that you really love.

In your sacred place you get the feeling of connection to life that the ancients had for the whole of the world in which they lived. This is a place of creative incubation.

2 Get comfortable

Sit on a chair or on the floor. Arrange your legs in the most comfortable position if sitting on the floor; if on a chair, sit with your legs uncrossed and your feet flat on the floor. Keep your back as straight as possible. Fold your hands comfortably in your lap.

3 Breathe

Now, take a deep breath and let it out slowly. Do the same again. Relax, and focus on the rise and fall of your chest. Your eyes will close of their own accord and your breathing will start to slow. Up to this point, you are practising a relaxation technique that is good for dealing with stress and you can use it for that at any time, even in the office.

4 Visualization

When you are relaxed, you can start the suggested visualization. Remember, you are in complete control of your experience and can stop at any time. This is not hypnosis or anything similar: it is just relaxation.

Chapter 1
Setting the scene: everyday life in ancient Egypt

It is rightly said that the 'Dawn of Conscience' occurred in ancient Egypt. There was belief in a 'Great God', the supreme deity from which all else came and from which came *Ma'at*, the quality of being in right-relationship with the surrounding world. There were the roots of morality and ethics, the idea that this life was a passage into the next and that what happened on that passage was determined by one's conduct in the here and now. These concepts were the anchor of Egyptian life and were well in place 5,000 years ago.

For countless millennia the Nile has found its way from the highlands of west-central Africa down to the Mediterranean. Through aeons it has cut its way through the roots of worn-down mountains and the solidified sands of ancient seas, rivers, and deserts. Along its course have lived *Arsinotherms*, rhinoceros-like animals with two side-by-side tusks, *Mastodonts*, the ancestors of mastodons and elephants and, finally, some of the earliest ancestors of human beings.

Upon these rocks and fossils and sands arose the premier civilization of the ancient world, Egypt. The birth of Egyptian civilization is shrouded in mystery. Egypt did not evolve in a step-by-step fashion but, rather, sprang full-blown from seemingly nowhere. There were already primitive people living in the Nile Valley; from about 10,000 BC to 5000 BC the peoples referred to as 'Predynastic' by archaeologists moved up and down the valley, leaving remains here and there. From the end of the last Ice Age the Nile valley attracted peoples from the Sahara and North Africa. Much of the valley at that time would have been inhospitable swamp, but as the Sahara dried out and became uninhabitable, the Nile's level also dropped, opening new and inviting areas for human living. But even at the beginning of the emergence of true Egyptian civilization these people were still largely Stone Age people, with little to suggest a civilization about to flower.

Any understanding of ancient Egypt must take into account the enormous timespans involved and their vastly different ways of thinking about things. And yet, people are still people, still largely motivated by the same things, still fearing the same fears and hoping the same basic hopes. Thus, this civilization, ancient even when Rome fell, has much to teach us about the art of being human.

In fact, even in Roman times there was much interest in the study of ancient Egypt. Wealthy Romans travelled to Egypt to view its monuments – already antiquities in those days. When Egypt became a province of Rome with the defeat of Anthony and Cleopatra, ancient Egyptian monuments and artifacts were carted away to Rome by the shipload. The obelisks called 'Cleopatra's Needle' in Paris and London are two of these – first taken by the Romans from Heliopolis to Roman Alexandria, and from there by the French and the British to their countries in the 1800s. After the fall of Rome and the descent of the Dark Ages, interest in Egypt faded away, but from the fifteenth to eighteenth centuries, there was a steady revival in Europe. As Europeans began to travel more widely, scholars began a more systematic study.

When Napoleon I conquered Egypt in 1798, he was accompanied by a team of scholars who began a comprehensive study. The Rosetta Stone, a stone bearing inscriptions in hieroglyphics, demotic – the cursive form of Egyptian writing – and Greek, was discovered. When the British defeated Napoleon, both Egypt and the Rosetta Stone were ceded to them. It was principally from work on this stone that Jean-François Champollion finally deciphered hieroglyphics in 1822. From that moment the writings and inscriptions were open to scholars.

In the first half of the 1800s Egypt was effectively plundered for antiquities by Europeans. Many of the major museum collections of today are formed around a nucleus of material obtained during that time. In fairness, archaeology as a science was yet to be developed, but much important information was lost and this is another reason for the gaps in our knowledge.

Egyptology as a science in and of itself was developed in France and Prussia. Britain became more involved as the nineteenth century drew to a close, with Sir Flinders Petrie spending more than 40 years excavating in Egypt. Britain's work in Egypt reached, quite literally, a golden pinnacle in 1922 with Howard Carter's discovery of the tomb of Tutankhamen.

Excavation and further surveying continues to this day, with many new and important finds appearing each year.

Life in ancient Egypt

The majority of people in ancient Egypt lived in towns and villages of mud-brick in the Nile Valley and Delta. The most favoured places for settlements were the slightly higher bits of land above the level of the annual Nile flooding. As the Nile overflow was increasingly channelled by settlers into overflow areas, much more land was available for settlement.

Most of the people were occupied in agriculture and were tied to the land. Ownership and use of land was complex. Although it all technically belonged to the pharaoh, those living and working on it had certain rights. Some land could be bought and sold, and land rights were not easily violated, even by officialdom. Some land was assigned to officials to provide them with income and most land required the payment of fees to the state. Because the principal wealth of Egypt was its rich harvests, keeping the land in agricultural use was a priority. Any land abandoned by its user was returned to the state and put back into agriculture.

Workers were tied to the land, but were not slaves. They paid a portion of their crops to the relevant official. A class of freemen who worked their own land eventually emerged. Hollywood epics nothwithstanding, slavery was not widespread. It was limited to foreign captives or to those forced by poverty to sell themselves into slavery. But even that was not final. Slaves were often assimilated by marriage and became free. Slaves undergoing punishment were often assigned to hazardous work such as mining and quarrying, however.

The actual geographical area of Egypt varied somewhat through history. In general, it was the Nile Valley – never more than a few miles wide, the Nile delta and the Faiyum, a large ancient lakebed and the remnants of its lake, south of modern Cairo. The southernmost boundary was usually the first cataract of the Nile, just south of Aswan, where the Kingdom of Nubia began. Parts of Nubia were incorporated into the Egyptian state from time to time, as were some of the surrounding regions where Egypt exerted special rights, such as mining.

The main portions of Egypt form what is basically an oasis in the desert, an oasis determined by the highs and lows of the Nile. In essence, Egypt was a country 450 km (300 miles) long and a few miles wide. On either side stretched endless desert, leaving Egypt in splendid isolation. It also provided great security, largely preventing the endless wars and destruction that were characteristic of most states in antiquity. Just how isolated is illustrated by texts from around 2500 BC from both Mesopotamia and Syria: Egypt is not even mentioned!

Rainfall in the Nile valley is almost non-existent and even in the delta it is minute. Without the Nile, agriculture, and thus the whole of Egyptian civilization, would have been impossible. The waters of the Nile rise in the Ethiopian highlands; the Blue Nile and the White Nile arise from dozens of small streams in southern Sudan and even as far as Lake Victoria in Uganda. The White Nile in particular, fed by the rains of the tropical belt, is responsible for the annual rise of waters and flooding. This annual inundation of the Nile Valley, starting in July and lasting through to October, with a peak in August, is the basis for the rich soil and hearty agriculture upon which Egypt grew rich and powerful. The year began with the rising of the star Sirius above the horizon, several weeks before the annual inundation of the Nile began during the season of *akhet*, corresponding to the period July to October. There were three seasons, each of four months. Ploughing and sowing took place during November to February and the harvest season was the period March to June. The calendar was lunar and accurate. The year lasted 365 days, with an extra day added every fourth year – just as the Western calendar today. Eventually, the Nile's overflow was carefully channelled to provide water and soil where desired and a great civil administration grew up around the overflow's management. This created a need for an expanded bureaucracy to administer the regions. In the earliest days, Egypt was essentially a personal estate of the pharaoh, but by 1500 BC it was divided into 35 administrative areas, each administered by its own officials. These administrative areas, known as *nomes*, existed from the first cataract to Memphis (modern Cairo). By 2000 BC the whole of Egypt had been precisely surveyed.

The holders of the highest offices were directly appointed by the pharaoh, based in large part on his theoretically superior judgements as a god. They were quick to sing their own praises in inscriptions, celebrating their exploits and offering themselves as ideals to be emulated. They were always quick to acknowledge the pharaoh as the source of all their prowess and, likewise, always had ample justifications for their behaviour toward their inferiors – especially that, aside from the pharaoh, they were the first to help themselves generously to the country's wealth. The main group of the wealthiest officeholders were a few hundred at most, and the minor officials numbered around 5,000.

Officials progressed up a complex career ladder, accumulating more wealth as they went up. At the top was the vizier, the chief administrator and the senior judge, who reported only to the pharaoh. The young were exhorted to become scribes. It was emphasised to them that the scribe was the supervisor while others did the hard work.

The priesthood was not separate until rather late in Egyptian history. The high office-holders were the priests – often for no better reason than it gave them a higher income. Until late in the New Kingdom, the state and religion were so intertwined there was no real distance between them. As they became more separate entities, tensions grew between them.

Organization of Egyptian society

Egyptian social organization was hierarchical, starting with the gods, then the pharaoh, the dead, and the rest of humanity – which would have been understood by most as just being other Egyptians. So isolated was Egypt for much of the time that only the vaguest awareness of the rest of the world existed for most.

The pharaoh was considered a god, but a god inferior to the other gods of the hierarchy. His divinity came with his job and the numerous religious rituals he was obliged to perform renewed and reaffirmed his divinity. He was, to other mortals, the direct representative of the gods on earth; and, to a lesser extent, he was humanity's representative to the gods.

The dead were considered to be capable of intervening in human affairs and the living were, therefore, obliged to render homage and service to them. Indeed, much of life for both pharaohs and mortals was in providing for the next world.

The pharaoh was originally an absolute monarch at the centre of a small ruling clique who were mostly his relatives. The pharaoh was individually more prominent than any of the others, and the text summarizes his role as being 'on earth for ever and ever, judging mankind and appeasing the gods, and setting order in place of disorder. He gives offerings to the gods and gives offerings to the blessed dead.' But as time progressed, he became more like a chief bureaucrat as Egypt grew and the governing body expanded. The increased management of the Nile and the need to divide its length into workable management districts was, in large part, responsible for this. He was still an absolute ruler, but tradition and personal connections became increasingly a limiting power on the ultimate authority of the pharaoh.

The word *pharaoh* is an Old Testament term and comes from the Egyptian *per 'aa*, meaning 'great estate', referring to the designation of the royal palace as the governing institution *per se*.

Writing

The Egyptian language is a member of the Afro-Asiatic or Hamito-Semitic family of languages. Its written forms were at the centre of the Egyptian state. Without it the central administration of such a large – or at least such a long – country would have been impossible. *Hieroglyphics* is the best-known type of writing, used mostly for inscriptions and display. But there was a second type, *hieratic* (meaning, literally: 'the writing of the priests'), a writing done with joined characters. They were both invented at about the same time – around 3000 BC. Writing was mainly used for administration for many hundreds of years, but eventually traditional material was written down, such as medical treatises, and the rituals of the afterlife: *The Book of the Dead*. As all but a few people were illiterate, there was no real impetus to develop literature.

Some of the earliest texts refer to a past 'golden age' that people living in the Egypt of the time of texts could only hope to imitate. It wasn't until the Middle Kingdom, starting about 2000 BC, that a wider range of subjects was written about. There are stories, dialogues, lamentations and plenty of instructions on how to live a good life. They paint a much richer picture of Egyptian life than the ritualized rhetoric of inscriptions.

There were treatises on mathematics, astronomy, medicine, magic and religious texts and lists that classified various categories of creation. One thing noticeable in all these texts is the lack of a systematic arrangement of material. Bits and pieces are scattered here and there throughout most texts. There are a few exceptions, such as a medical treatise on wounds, some very accomplished texts on surveying, planning and orienting buildings to fine tolerances, and for the regular division of agricultural lands after each inundation.

Agriculture

Because the Egyptians used no money, trade revolved principally around grain. The economy's central functions were the collection, storage and distribution of produce, and the management and organization of labour, especially in the one large and central public-works project: the Nile. The fertility of the soil provided for huge harvests and a healthy surplus to be stored against crop failures.

The main crops were: cereals – emmer for bread and barley for beer – lentils and chickpeas, lettuce, onions, garlic, fruit and dates. Loaves were the staple form of carbohydrate and the baking process converted the grains into many valuable nutrients. Yeast was used in the dough, which was baked, soaked in water and fermented. A by-product of this process within the loaf was the antibiotic tetracycline which, doubtless, added to the health of people living in essentially unsanitary conditions. Sesame was grown for oil and bees were extensively kept for honey. Meat was a rarity in the average diet, but, when available, beef was the most prized, although mutton, pork and goat were also eaten. The food of the rich was fowl. Fish was vital in just about everyone's diet.

Papyrus grew wild and abundant in the marshes and was later cultivated. It was used to make rope, mats and sandals. And, of course, paper. In later Egypt it became Egypt's chief export, along with grain.

The domestication of animals proceeded apace in ancient Egypt. Cattle, which may have originally been domesticated in the area, were used less for meat and more as draft animals, and for their various products. There was deliberate breeding, not only of cattle, but of other species as well. The donkey, the principal form of transport, was probably domesticated and bred there. The principal meat-animal was sheep.

Pets were widely kept and included dogs, monkeys and, of course, cats which were domesticated in Egypt. There was a widespread interest in animals in the environment and there was considerable knowledge of mammals, birds, fish, and reptiles.

Minerals

To the east of Egypt, in the Sinai, were important sources of minerals. Turquoise and copper were especially prized. It is likely that the Egyptians didn't mine the minerals themselves, but rather the mines were worked by local people under Egyptian control. Obsidian and lapis-lazuli were imported from as far away as

Anatolia and Afghanistan. The eastern desert of Egypt itself was an important source of semi-precious stones and stone for carving. There were also gold mines which could not have been exploited without Egyptian domination of the area. Control was also needed of this area for access to the Red Sea, of which there were three main routes. Thus, when we think of Egypt we must also think of the areas which Egypt either controlled or dominated.

Nubia

There is one more area that needs to be mentioned – Nubia. The lands south of the first cataract was referred to as 'Nubia' in Egyptian texts and, although it was referred to as a separate state, there seems to have been a belief that Egypt had certain rights of domination there. At times, Nubia was more or less incorporated into the Egyptian state and at others it was yielded back to the local inhabitants.

It was an important area economically and a rich source of gold and carving stone. Many of the famous Egyptian statues are carved from Nubian stone. It was an important source of wood and it was equally important as a trade route for other African goods. Spice, ebony, ivory and ostrich feathers were prized imports. Baboons and pygmies seem to have been traded with about equal status as goods! These imported goods were high-status goods and were often for religious use.

Egyptian history

The following paragraphs contain a brief history of Egypt. For reasons that will be explained more fully later, the time period that concerns us the most is the earliest days of Egyptian civilization. At that time the new impulse which created Egypt was at its freshest. The actual day-to-day history is much less important than what took place within the culture – the wisdom of Egypt that has passed down to us through the ages.

There is, in fact, no accurate political history of Egypt. Evidence comes mostly from inscriptions, where there are large gaps and confusing overlaps, caused in part by the method of numbering according to reignal years. Because inscriptions, especially early on, related only to the pharaoh, his recording of his reign was not to record history as we think of it today, but to record his accomplishments in serving the gods. In the Egyptian view, the pharaoh is the establisher of order and the re-creator of the world. The year was most often incidental to the event recorded.

Dates used by Egyptians were those of the years of the reign of a particular pharaoh. When the next pharaoh was crowned, the dates started all over again. There was no accumulated dating system, as we have now; that is, from the birth of Christ as in the Christian calendar.

Predynastic Egypt

The peoples of predynastic Egypt were the successors of the Stone Age peoples of north-eastern Africa, who migrated to the Nile Valley as the Sahara dried up. Sometime after 5000 BC the small-scale raising of crops began. The material culture improved toward the end of the period, with good-quality pottery depicting scenes of people, boats and animals. Flint was worked with great skill to produce beautiful ceremonial knives, as well as more utilitarian objects.

The Thinite Period

Sometime around 3200 BC a dramatic change took place. In a short period of time, writing appeared, Egypt was united under a single king, a bureaucratic administrative system was introduced and an elaborate social system grew rapidly. All without any obvious development stages. Within a relatively few years, objects from the new Egypt scarcely bore any resemblance to similar objects from the old Egypt.

The Old Kingdom (c.3000 BC—c.2280 BC)

Archaeologists divide dynastic from predynastic Egypt as the point where the written records start to include the years of the pharaoh's reign. This is an artificial division as, in fact, the cultural upheaval that changed the face of Egypt forever had taken place over 100 years before. Indeed, for the purpose of this book, we will understand that the beginning of the Egypt we are interested in was, without doubt, about 3200 BC, king-years or not. There is little written evidence preserved from this time and the earliest more-or-less complete material is the Pyramid Texts, described later in this book, dating from about 2500 BC.

The First Intermediate Period (c.2280 BC–c.2050 BC)

This was a time of social revolution when royal power was weakened.

The Middle Kingdom (c.2050 BC–c.1780 BC)

Most of the earliest written material passed down to us comes from this period. The political centre of Egypt had moved to Thebes.

The Second Intermediate Period (c.1780 BC–c.1570 BC)

Egypt went into serious decline. Peoples from Asia, the Hyskos, subjugated Egypt and many 'foreign' influences were injected into Egyptian thought and religion at this time. This is why the periods before are most important as far as this book is concerned. The purity of early Egyptian wisdom was diluted and changed during this period.

The New Kingdom (c.1570 BC–c.1080 BC)

After throwing off the foreign yoke, there was a great resurgence of Egyptian life. It was Egypt's greatest period of expansion. The Exodus took place during this period and Tutankhamen was a minor pharaoh of the eighteenth dynasty.

The Late Period (c.1080 BC–330 BC)

This period saw the terminal decline of Egypt. Egypt was conquered by the Assyrians and the Persians and, finally, by the Greeks under Alexander the Great. After 330 BC Egypt was ruled by Greeks and finally became a province of Rome after the fall of Anthony and Cleopatra, the last Greek ruler being in 30 BC. Although Egyptian thought and religion played a significant role in the Roman Empire, and even influenced early Christianity to an important degree, it was the end of over 3,000 years of successful civilization.

Much of the written record of Egypt comes from this later period, from the time of the Greek conquest. But it is thoroughly interspersed with Greek thought and is of little value in assessing true Egyptian wisdom, the wisdom of the first impulse that in a short time transformed a primitive people into the greatest civilization of the ancient world.

Chapter 2
The mystery begins: pyramids

The subject of pyramids has fascinated people for thousands of years. In Roman times travellers made special trips to Egypt to see them, and writers throughout history have speculated about them. Even in Cleopatra's time the pyramids were immensely ancient; just how ancient has been a source of much modern speculation. Within the last few years a number of books have appeared that suggest that the Giza pyramids, and the Great Pyramid in particular, are vastly older than Egyptologists believe. Another recent study by geologists of the Great Sphinx, which lies at the foot of the Giza pyramids, suggests that it was, in antiquity, weathered by water. As the Giza plateau was part of the general drying out of the Sahara about 10,000 years ago, to have been weathered by water it must be nearly that old – if, indeed, not older.

The number of books written about the pyramids would make a small pyramid themselves, and this book can do little to resolve any of the numerous arguments put forward. But without a doubt there is a message to be read in the pyramids, whether it is a message from immense antiquity as some suggest, or whether they were the creation of the Egyptians themselves in the Old Kingdom, in the Pyramid Age, as suggested by academic Egyptologists.

The mother mountain

Mountains as dwelling places of divinities have been a common theme among most human cultures. The Indians of North and South America revered certain mountains and the Incas in Peru even sacrificed small children to them. Within the last decades, their bodies, mummified by the cold and dry air at the high altitudes of the sacred peaks, have been found. In ancient Greece, the gods lived on Mount Olympus and Moses brought down the Ten Commandments from Mount Sinai. The list goes on.

Where there wasn't a mountain handy, artificial mountains were built: the ziggurats of Mesopotamia, the most famous of which was the Tower of Babel; Silbury Hill in England; the pyramids built in the southern United States, Mexico and, of course, in Egypt.

It is possible that the first pyramids in Egypt were created as the primordial hillock where the god Re stood when he created the first land from the swirling wastes of water. It is even possible that if the Great Pyramid is, indeed, the first pyramid, and existed as early as 10,000 to 12,000 BC as some researchers suggest, then this may have been believed by later Egyptians to be *literally* the primordial hillock. The second possibility is that the pyramids were built later and became symbolic of the primordial mountain. With the state of Egyptology at the moment, both formal and informal, it is impossible to be certain, but there are plenty of theories to choose from. Of all of these, Pyramidology is the grandfather.

Pyramidology

Pyramidology emerged from a theory proposed by Englishman John Taylor in 1859 and was championed and further developed by the Astronomer Royal, Charles Smith. In 1864 Smith proposed that the Great Pyramid was built to embody certain facets of ancient knowledge, knowledge that was highly advanced. The first proposition was that the pyramid is unique among the monuments of ancient Egypt and that it was built under divine inspiration by a highly advanced race of invaders.

Not only that but both the biblical Israelites and the Anglo-Saxons were their descendants. To pass on the message of the pyramid to future ages, it was built to certain precise mathematical proportions in order that future ages might believe its message, that encoded within its various measurements were prophecies of future events, events which would form the basis of the Old Testament, the future history of Christianity and the Second Coming of Christ. The pyramid was built to attract our attention, in part by embodying the mathematical number Pi, which is the ratio of the circumference of a circle to its radius, and that its measurements were obviously built around a high degree of astronomical knowledge and knowledge of the earth's surface. Whether or not the pyramidologist's interpretations are true there are some definite modern discoveries that have a bearing on 'pyramid power'.

Inside the pyramid

We are only just beginning to discover the complex range of electromagnetic, gravitational and radiation influences to which human life is subjected. One often-reported experience inside the Great Pyramid is that the rules of time and space on the inside are somehow different from on the outside. When the geometry of the pyramid is combined with the shielding effect of its bulk, the likelihood of a noticeable effect is considerable. The forces involved may or may not be measurable to science, but then many of the most important forces still are not.

For example, we are only just beginning to understand the effect of electromagnetic fields on the human body. The first concrete discoveries were made in 1952 by a German scientist, Professor W. O. Schumann, who identified waves of very low frequency associated with the earth's own magnetic and electrical field. These waves may well be generated between the inner and outer core of the earth. The outer core is molten and, therefore, some 'slippage' occurs as the earth rotates, between the outer part of the earth and the inner core. This would have the effect of a dynamo, generating not only the magnetic field, but other energies as well. The total mineral make-up of the earth would have a great deal of effect on exactly which waves are generated.

Professor Schumann suggested that these waves may influence all life. In fact, it probably goes far beyond that – life as it evolved on the earth would have evolved in harmony with these waves. Any creatures attempting to evolve that were not in harmony with them, would have died out.

Important evidence about the earth's wave effects came from some of the first manned space flights – flights at a distance from the earth where the wave effects were much reduced. Astronauts returned feeling distressed and disorientated – until devices for generating Schumann waves were installed in the spacecraft. Schumann waves pulse almost within the same frequency as brainwaves – between 1 and 30 Hz. Jet lag may be a result of being shielded by the plane's metallic casing, and flying at an altitude where Schumann waves are considerably weaker. It is usually made worse by moving to a place where the waves are pulsing at a different point in their 24-hour rhythm. For example, stewardesses on long-haul duty often experience irregular periods and may stop menstruating altogether. It is highly likely that such waves would be blocked or modified, or both, by the bulk and geometry of the pyramid.

There is another unknown energy that directly affects us, which may be blocked or altered by the pyramid. One of the most startling early discoveries about human interconnection with the outer rhythms of the world was that the clotting rate of blood varies directly with both sunrise and with the appearance of sunspots. A Japanese physician, Maki Takata, discovered that the flocculation index (a measure of the clotting rate) varied throughout the day, becoming very low at night and suddenly rising rapidly at the coming of day. The rise actually begins before sunrise as if the blood 'knows' the sunrise is coming.

But how do we know the rise is directly related to the blood's 'sensing' the rising sun? To test this several people were taken to places where a full eclipse of the sun was to take place, a place where whatever solar effects there might be would be blocked out by the moon. Sure enough, as the eclipse progressed the flocculation index dropped, rising again as the eclipse ended. It is still unknown which solar radiation produces the effect, or how the blood senses it, but it is powerful enough to penetrate almost everything except the moon and, obviously, the earth itself, as the index drops during the hours of darkness when the sun is behind the earth. The effect has been observed everywhere, except in one test that was done well underground in a mine! [1] One place is hasn't been tried yet is inside a pyramid, but the outcome of it is unlikely to surprise anyone.

The point of these examples is that, aside from the more esoteric interpretations of what goes on inside pyramids, there are real and identifiable effects. When we realise that we have yet to discover many of the energies that affect our lives and the world around us, it would come as no surprise whatever that pyramids alter them as well. When science is ready to find them, within and around the pyramids is a good place to start looking for their effects.

The symbolism of pyramids

The Great Pyramid, apart from any interpretative considerations, is noted for the precise orientation of its sides to the four cardinal points of the compass. Even if it was built around 2500 BC as academic Egyptologists suggest, there would have been a high significance to the alignment. Precise compass alignments are part and parcel of many ancient structures from many cultures. For example, the native American 'medicine wheels' were always precisely oriented because of the belief that there were sacred attributes to each of the four directions. There was a similar belief in Egypt, where each of the four cardinal directions had its own god. These gods were called the *Tchatcha*. They were instrumental in the passing of the soul from life into the realm of Osiris, in that their opposition to the passing was enough to prevent it. Thus, in any structure dedicated to the afterlife they would surely have some important architectural counterpart – if, indeed, that is what the Great Pyramid was.

Time after time in past-life regressions, the pyramids have emerged not as places of burial, but as places of initiation. Indeed, they may have come to be burial places, but that was not the original intent. Especially if we view the pyramids as 'mother

[1] Gauquelin, 1967, p. 155.

mountains', as the places of the gods, does their significance as places of initiation emerge. The trinity, as represented by the triangular faces of the pyramid, has always been a powerful symbol in human understanding. As the local gods of Egypt began to intermix with and supplant each other, we find groupings of three gods the norm at most temples: two older, 'mature' gods and one 'younger' god. Entering a pyramid may well have been experienced as entering the realm of the gods.

Initiation has always been about testing one's right-relationship with the surrounding universe. In Egypt, this right-relationship was called *Ma'at*. In the pyramid we have each of the attributes of the four cardinal directions expressed through the three fundamental aspects of Self: Love, Power and Wisdom, represented as a triangle, the pyramid's sides. These are the three segments of Ma'at that must be in right-relationship and such would have been tested inside the pyramid. The pyramid then, is the four triangles of self-completion. When the three sides are equal (i.e. in right-relationship) it is the strongest form in the universe, and a person who manifests the three aspects in equal measure is Self fulfilled. It is when the three aspects are not in equal measure that the person is out of balance, out of harmony with his or her inner nature. At each turn of the cycle of life is a new opportunity to strengthen each of these aspects and, equally, a risk of imbalance – such is the challenge of growth. It is as true today as it was 5,000 years ago and is an important legacy of ancient Egyptian wisdom.

The three aspects can be perhaps best illustrated by looking at those who manifest their unbalanced extremes.

- **The Power type** You have seen them; you read about them every day. People who seek power for its own sake, people who use it without the wisdom to use it properly and who lack the love to care about the destructive results of their exercise of it. Stalin was a classic example of this type. There is nothing wrong with power – it is just that we have mostly experienced it in its unbalanced form. Indeed, you couldn't walk across a room without the power of your muscles. And without the power to bring love and wisdom into the world, both are unfocused and dispersed ineffectually.

- **The Love type** Many flower-power people of the 1970s illustrated this type: genuinely full of love, but lacking the wisdom or the power to bring it into manifestation – floating around in a lovely haze of love, but without much else happening.
- **The Wisdom type** This type is the guru on the mountain top full of the wisdom of the ages, but without the love to bring his wisdom down into the market place for others to share.

As we can imagine, each of these types of separation has its own seductions, its own excuses for being separate from the other two. As we progress through our exploration of ancient Egyptian wisdom, keep these three aspects in mind. Although it will not be pointed out at each stage, one or more of these aspects will be present in each dimension of ancient wisdom we uncover.

Visualization

The pyramid visualizations

The pyramid is the singularly most powerful of Egyptian images. Pyramids combine the symbolism of the Mother Mountain with the primordial womb in their inner chambers. Thus as an archetypal symbol for use in visualization, they are unsurpasssed for tapping into ancient Egyptian wisdom. Several of the visualizations will use pyramids and all will follow the same general format as below. The human mind works by creating appropriate symbols that our subconscious mind will grasp quickly. Our mind makes the perceptual shifts that are necessary for our further personal growth.

Setting things in motion

This meditation uses the inner sanctum of the pyramid as a metaphor for the deepest inner self, where all change begins.

1 To start, close your eyes and find yourself standing at the head of an avenue lined on both sides with sphinxes, which leads to the entrance of a pyramid. You are dressed in

initiation robes and are accompanied by a group of softly chanting priests. It is a time of initiation, of going inward, to speak to the deepest level of your own being and to create intentions for your growth and expansion as a fully realised Being.

2 At the sound of a gong, the moment has come to start your journey. As you walk towards the pyramid, you are aware of the soft, warm breeze and, with the exception of the soft chanting and the sound of your sandals on the stone pathway, the utter stillness.

3 As you reach the ramp leading up into the pyramid, the chanting stops and you proceed alone. The corridor into the centre of the pyramid is lit with torches and, as you enter, the cool stone surrounds you. As you walk further inwards, you reach the doorway to the inner chamber and enter.

4 The chamber is lit by a single candle and waiting for you is the High Priest or Priestess, dressed in the feather robe of Osiris. He/she wordlessly directs you to the gold-gilt chair in the exact centre of the chamber, where you sit. He/she kneels before you and anoints your forehead with fragrant oils.

His/her words to you, echoing around the chamber, are simple: 'May you find what you seek.' Then he/she exits silently, leaving you alone.

5 As you sit quietly, begin to sense the expanse of the pyramid around you, and then the world beyond it. It will take on an actual physical sensation, as if you yourself have expanded and are more connected to all that surrounds you. It is through this connection to the surrounding world that life is able to know and respond to our deepest needs. Remember that life responds to our real needs and not necessarily to our wishes and desires. Thus your intention in this moment of deeper connection will be that life fulfils your need for inner knowing, of the universal truths that are the true foundation of Egyptian belief, and of *all* true belief. Take all the time you need for this step.

6 Know that the path to the truth is an unfolding process and life will provide you only with whatever serves you best at the time. It may appear that nothing has happened, but don't worry – life never refuses a request for truth.

7 When you feel a sense of completion with the process, take a few deep breaths and become aware of your surroundings again. When you are ready, your eyes will open naturally.

In the following chapters, we will begin to explore some of the myths and symbols through which life communicates some of its most profound truths.

Chapter 3
The 'Great God': Egyptian religion

In virtually every culture the highest wisdoms of that culture are embodied in its religious thought. But in examining Egyptian religion, we encounter a stumbling block. Most readers will come from the Western tradition of thought which is, quite literally, a pole apart from Eastern thought. This polarity of thought will be examined in more detail later as it will be essential to the unravelling of Egyptian wisdom. But suffice it to say for the moment that Egyptian thought, wisdom and religion is much more Eastern than Western in its outlook. In many respects it resembles classic Hinduism. This is not a barrier to understanding Egyptian wisdom, but it will require the reader to have an open mind about some of the concepts described here.

The oldest written records of Egyptian belief are religious texts, called the Pyramid Texts. They are inscribed in hieroglyphics inside several of the pyramids at Sakkara. They date to about 2500 BC, but it is clear that they contain material that originates much further back in time. They contain myths, burial rituals, hymns, incantations and magic spells. They are, in fact, the earliest body of religious writings in the whole of humanity. It is important to realize that although they are *preserved* from this time, they constitute an elaborate and complete theology and must have been passed down through many, many generations. Although they speak of creation itself, and the belief that the world and humans emerged from a primordial waste of water (sounding suspiciously like the knowledge that all life evolved in and from the sea), they are mostly concerned with the afterlife of the pharaohs buried there.

As we will discover in this chapter, there was a great deal of confusing intermixture of belief as time progressed and it is already beginning to show in the Pyramid Texts. It is one of the main reasons why, when we look for the real roots of Egyptian belief, we must look at a much earlier time.

Like the Pyramid Texts, the Egyptian *Book of the Dead* relates not to life, but to afterlife. *The Book of the Dead* is a title used by modern Egyptologists – the Egyptians called it *Chapters for Going Forth by Day*. The afterlife was believed to be a place requiring careful navigation through a number of pitfalls, many of which could be magically avoided by the correct rituals. Both of these texts were directed towards the pharaoh, and 'the common man' did not figure in them at all.

Gods, gods and more gods

Looking at the full range of Egyptian religious beliefs and practice over 3,000 years presents us with a bewildering hodgepodge of animism, monotheism, pantheism and downright confusion. But we have a similar situation with religious belief today, from which parallels may be drawn. In the first instance Christians, Muslims and Jews are all 'People of the Book'; that is, with a common history expressed in the Old Testament. Only the least enlightened of any of those religions seriously believe that the god of each of those religions is not the same god, whatever name we use for him. Or, that each of those religions worships him in accord with his attributes expressed by that particular religion. But what would happen in 2,000 years if most records were lost? Would people then see them as three different gods?

And to take the single example of Christianity as it has progressed over the last 2,000 years: there are and have been a number of 'Christianities'. There have been and are Gnostics,

Catholics, Protestants, Baptists, Methodists, Eastern Orthodox and even Mormons. Not to mention the local varieties of Christianity in Polynesia, Mexico and South and Central America, and Africa where it has taken on, to varying degrees, aspects of the previous culture and beliefs. So if we were to study 'Christianity', where would we begin? Obviously, we would go back as far into the past, as near to the origins of Christianity as possible. So too, shall we do with Egyptian religion. For there is evidence that about 3200 BC a religious surge infused the various tribes of the Nile Valley with a single, unifying impulse. Where many local beliefs existed, the new force changed and modified, and in many instances replaced the old. From all of this, Egyptian religion was created.

Strange gods?

Although from the outside it might appear that the Egyptians worshipped a whole host of strange-looking gods – gods with bird's or ram's or crocodile's heads – we must be careful not to take these too literally. Most importantly because the expression 'the Great God' appears quite frequently; although nowhere is the Great God described or given a name, the frequent use of the term is highly important. The Egyptians recognized one supreme deity who was so well known and accepted by all that he[1] needed no special name. Because we are dealing exclusively with ancient written sources, we must understand that if something was 'common knowledge', no one saw any need to write it down. This happens not only with religious texts, but with other writings as well. It is true that this Great God became associated with Re the sun god early on, and with other gods like Amun and Aten later, there was still a clear distinction.

Second, it is likely that the other 'gods' were like totems in their attributes. That is to say, that the animal represents an attribute of the Great God that an individual could identify with.

---

[1] Although referred to here as 'he' in keeping with Western tradition, the Egyptians recognized that the Great God was beyond gender. In Chapter 4 we will look at understandings of human life based on both male and female god-figures, but keep in mind that above the god and goddess figures in Egyptian mythology was the Great God, of which all gods and goddesses were a part.

Native American tribes in the north-west recognized the Great Spirit, yet identified with an animal that represented some aspect of this spirit. There are even metaphors in Christianity that would be very confusing to a future archaeologist. For example, Christ is referred to as 'The Lamb of God'. Another Christian symbol is the fish, and in communion services we are invited to partake in the blood and flesh of Christ. These are all perfectly clear meanings today, but what would people 2,000 years in the future think if most of our written records were lost? Certainly the latter could be taken to suggest cannibalism!

Too, there is ample evidence from many ancient cultures that various birds, animals and even insects became 'familiars' in shamanic practice. That is, the shaman was able to (in theory at least) either directly embody or even occupy the body of a particular bird or animal for the purpose of reaching different levels of existence in order to bring back wisdom for the benefit of his group. There are a number of suggestive Egyptian writings and inscriptions that use animal imagery relating to the gods. From *The Book of the Dead*, for example, we find the dead pharaoh joining Re: 'He flieth as a bird, and he settleth as a beetle...' These references may certainly be translated as metaphors; but there is evidence that suggests shamanic elements were part of religious practice.

Another point to consider about Egyptian animal-gods is that many of them were local gods. It would be a mistake to think of 'The Egyptians' as a single, homogenous people. There were many tribes scattered along the length of the Nile that eventually became incorporated into the Egyptian state and, just as with any large society today, there was a mixture of ideas and beliefs. Without a doubt, some of these groups would have had animistic beliefs. Thus in Egypt we find essentially two tiers of gods: powerful gods that were recognized just about everywhere and local gods. As time went on some of the local gods gained prominence for a time, then declined, then others arose and declined.

By the beginning of the New Kingdom, about 1500 BC, local gods were so much in demand that an attempt to create a one-god religion ended in disaster for the pharaoh involved.

Amenophis IV came to the throne in about 1350 BC and gradually set about supplanting the then supreme god Amun (who started his career as a local god) with Aten. He moved his capital from Thebes, the centre of Amun worship, and built an entirely new capital called Ankhetaten ('Horizon of the Aten'). He changed his own name to Ankhenaten ('Pleasing to the Aten'), closed temples to other gods, and had Amun's name removed from inscriptions across Egypt. He was married to the beautiful Nefertiti and had several children with her. Within a brief time after his death, virtually the whole of Aten worship collapsed and his capital was abandoned and ravaged. Nefertiti ruled briefly, and then the son of a secondary wife succeeded her. He moved the capital back to Thebes and took a name meaning 'pleasing to the Amun' – Tutankhamun. The role of Ankhenaten is difficult to assess, although many books have been written on the subject. But it might be fair to say that the scarcity of written material from the time leaves room for doubt whether he intended true monotheism, or whether in creating solely one god, to whom he was conveniently the high priest, he was merely indulging in megalomaniac self-glorification.

Degeneration of religious practice

Looking at the longer-term practices, we can see a degeneration over the centuries, as Egyptian religion separated itself from the earliest founders. Therefore, as we explore Egyptian religion in this book, we will be looking for the Great God and the universal wisdom intertwined with his myths and legends. The earliest impulse of any new religion is inevitably the purest, coming as it does from the personal revelation of its founder or founders. As time passes so, too, do the founders and their revelation then becomes interpreted and reinterpreted by those who follow, but who have not themselves had the revelation. Because teachings are always passed down the ages in words, there is always a gap between the truth of the revelation and its description – for the simple reason that it is the nature of spiritual revelation to be beyond words. Thus, as words become interpreted by others, various interpretations appear and beliefs grow up around them. Over many centuries the original vision is lost and only widely varying interpretations remain. When we understand that the original revelation of all religions is from the same source in all instances, we can begin to look at the earliest revelations and discover that whatever setting they are placed in, their basic elements are all the same. The lesser local deities generally appear much later in Egyptian belief than the archetypal stories of Isis and Osiris. There is a parallel in modern times: Christianity has split itself into three general divisions, Catholic, Eastern Orthodox and Protestant. But within those divisions are yet more divisions, each claiming some more accurate version or interpretation of the original events. To truly understand the original revelation of Christianity we cannot study any of these. We must go back to the original revelation and teaching.

Because in ancient time it was the fashion to cast revelations in stories of mythology, we can examine the myths to glean the universal truths behind them. This we shall do in the following chapter, but for the moment we will follow the course of Egyptian religion as the original revelation was lost.

Egyptian culture was almost entirely built around religion. Most of the written history of early Egypt – inscriptions, writings, monuments – is a religious history. Even later, when the commercial economy of Egypt blossomed, it was still organized with the temples at its centre.

Religion in Egypt came in two distinct forms: the official state religion and burial practices, about which we know quite a lot, and the workaday practices and beliefs of the vast majority of Egyptians, the peasants, about which we know relatively little. As in modern times, the official church and its practices are very different from the everyday practices of most people. The hierarchical nature of Egyptian life was such that the lower party in the pecking order might only offer humble service to those above, and had to be a passive recipient of whatever his betters condescended to bestow.

There was quite a language built up around the relationship between the pharaoh and the gods. The pharaoh or an ordinary moral cannot 'love' a god, but may only offer them 'respect' or 'adoration', or may offer them 'thanks'. The relationship between the pharaoh and the gods was more or less a commercial transaction. The pharaoh made an offering to the god or gods, from which he expected a return. One inscription states: 'The king has come to you (the god) bringing offerings which he has given to you, so that you may give to him all lands (or a similar gift)'.

In its inception, the idea that the leader of a people should intercede with the gods on their behalf is hardly a bad one. It would seem to go with the job. But as with many things that start out to be good in the beginning, a degeneration set in. Before long the pharaoh interceded with the gods only on behalf of himself as a lesser god, and never on behalf of the people.

As the temples grew in power and the priesthood extended its influence, changes took place. Temple practices were the preserve of the local priesthood and were not for the benefit of ordinary people. Even during festivals when the statue of the local god was brought out of the temple so ordinary people could approach it, it was kept hidden away in a portable shrine, not to be seen by mere mortals.

Ordinary people had their local shrines and lesser gods to whom they prayed and made offerings, or to lesser shrines of the main gods. These local shrines were also places of pilgrimage. As with the pharaoh, prayers and offerings were presented to the gods as a business transaction with expectations of a specific return: 'I'll offer you a sheep if you'll get me a better house' … and so on.

As the original meanings were forgotten, genuine animal worship took place in both official and ordinary religious practice. Certain animals became sacred to particular gods and were even ceremonially buried. This practice increased in later times. Animals were routinely mummified and, to pay for an animal's burial was considered a sacred deed. Animals were even farmed specially for this. Bulls, ibises, dogs, jackals, baboons, rams, snakes, fish, crocodiles and cats all discovered the benefits of mummification! In fact, an entire cemetary consisting of nothing but thousands of mummified cats has been discovered. Again, these practices took place in later Egyptian life and may be seen as a degeneration and failed understanding of the earliest religious impulse.

As time progressed, much religious practice became more or less magical. There are numerous texts that prescribe various rituals and practices for curing illness, finding love, divination through dreams, avoiding the evil eye, and ways of placating the dead who were thought to hold power over the living. Amulets and charms were popular, and included objects to be worn, those with special magical inscriptions, busts of ancestors kept in the home, and even special types of clothing to be worn for childbirth, etc.

Early beliefs

At the time of the Old Kingdom, there were three major religious centres: Heliopolis, Memphis and Hermopolis, each devoted to a different god. There was a uniform consensus among them regarding Creation, however. First, the god brought forth life. Then, there was a 'Golden Age', a time when laws, morals and institutions were given to humankind. This basic pattern of creation was repeated in the myths of most cultures of the time: the Tibetans, the Mayas, the Mesopotamians. In one of the Egyptian creation myths, man was created from clay, and the god breathed life into what he created – an echo of the Old Testament. But it is still a recognition that humans are of the Earth, literally. The archetypal story that was the most popular came from Heliopolis, the oldest religious centre – the story of Isis and Osiris. It is also significant that at Heliopolis was preserved the tradition that in the beginning there was only a primordial wasteland of water, from which all land and life arose – an understanding that all life arose from the sea.

The cult of the sun was developed very early on at Heliopolis, with the god Re, the sun, at its centre. He became a central figure in several myths, where some have him as the father of Osiris. Some of the pharaohs included the title 'son of Re' in their lineages. Although Re was the 'senior' god, there was still the recognition that above all gods was the Great God.

The ka, the ba and the ib

Religions are not just about cosmologies and gods and manifestations; they are concerned most of all with human nature and the destinies of men. The usual understanding of life in Egypt, was that the life being lived was in essence just a preparation for the life to come, for the life beyond the grave.[2] The interpretation of this understanding has been largely made by Western Egyptologists from the three Western religions, religions who see there being just one life, followed by an afterlife somewhere else – the 'else' depending on how you lived the one life.

But from the standpoint of reincarnation and Eastern teachings, the various dimensions that were understood by the Egyptians to make up life, make more sense.

One dimension was, of course, the physical. To have a life, you have to have a body. For a soul living on the earth, this is essentially true. That is the whole point of living on the earth in the first place.

Another dimension was created at conception, which was, essentially, an exact replica of the individual. This was called the *ka*. In Eastern thought this might be referred to as the etheric body, the energy field upon which the physical body is patterned. The Egyptians understood that the ka was non-material and was a vital force essential to the person's existence.

As the old meanings had been forgotten, and rituals were practised with little or no understanding of their true meaning or origin, the tomb became known as 'the house of the ka', the *het ka*. It eventually was believed that the ka continued to live on inside the tomb, hence the need for elaborate tomb preparation. 'To go to one's ka' became a euphemism for death.

There was another dimension to life also – the *ba*. This was believed to be an entity that separated from the body at death

---

[2] The Egyptians also believed that the dead have an influence on the lives of the living. While not specifically stated anywhere, this appears to correspond with the modern beliefs in angels or spirit guides or guardian angels, who are often the souls of the 'departed'.

and hovered nearby. It was usually represented as a human-headed bird. Again, the Egyptians were near the mark by Eastern standards. In many burial practices today, it is understood that the departed spirit, or soul, or atman, or whatever name it is given, stays near the body for three days after death. Even Western psychics are able to see, speak to, and be directed by this entity during that period. This has been well-attested in hundreds of instances.

The *ib* was perhaps the most important dimension of the person. The ib was connected to the heart and was referred to as 'the god in man'. We would now call it the residing place of the Higher Self, the eternal dimension that bears loving witness to the events of that particular lifetime. And, the residing place of the Source of all Being. After death, it was the ib that was weighed against Ma'at.

The Weighing of the Heart

One understanding that seems to have passed through the ages more or less intact was The Weighing of the Heart. For most of humanity (the pharaoh seems to have largely been excluded, since he was more or less a god anyway) at death there was a time of judgement, a sort of purgatory, in which the deeds of the just-finished life were weighed. The judgement itself was usually depicted as the weighing of the person's heart against the Egyptian concept of Ma'at, the 'right order' of life. Ma'at is most often depicted as a feather. This is a curiously insubstantial symbol, given that Ma'at was the absolute centre of Egyptian life. It is likely that it is a deliberate reference, acknowledging that the 'right order' of things is a very insubstantial thing, although very strong, and it is something that we can only sense in our hearts. Today we express Ma'at as the quality of being in right-relationship with all life around us.

Present at the weighing is Osiris, whose death, resurrection and ascent to the realm of the gods to sit as judge at God's right hand parallels that of Jesus. Also present is Thoth, who is the recorder – perhaps the Egyptian equivalent of the keeper of the Akashic Records in modern Eastern thought. If the heart and

Ma'at are perfectly balanced, the deceased is permitted to join Osiris. There were magical ways around a negative judgement and often inscriptions and offerings in the tomb were for this purpose. For those who failed, there was a female monster called The Eater of Souls; you definitely didn't want to meet *her*.

But Eaters of Souls aside, there is still the inherent recognition that the source of all Being resides in the heart and that the purity, or lack of it, in the person's heart is the determinant of the soul's further pathway.

The path of the heart is the path of the individual, but the path of Egyptian religion itself was governed by a higher awareness. The individual's heart will be explored in a later chapter, but now it is necessary to understand why the myths of Isis and Osiris, of Nut and Geb and the others, are at the heart of Egyptian wisdom. In Chapter 4 mythology itself is examined, for it is the tool by which the wisdom of ancient Egypt is extracted from its myths.

Visualization

Experiencing the 'Great God'

1 To start, close your eyes and find yourself again standing at the head of the avenue of sphinxes, leading to the entrance of a pyramid. You are dressed in heavy initiation robes, for it is the hour before sunrise, and the desert air is still chilly.
2 The moment has come to start your journey. As you walk alone towards the pyramid, you are aware of the soft, slightly damp breeze coming up from the Nile and, with the exception of the sound of your sandals on the stone pathway, the utter stillness.
3 You reach the ramp leading up into the pyramid and enter. The corridor into the centre of the pyramid is lit with torches and the cool stone surrounds you. As you walk further inwards, you reach the doorway to the inner chamber and enter. At the far side of this chamber is a hidden door, which the Doorkeeper silently opens upon your arrival. It leads to a spiral staircase which, in turn, leads

upwards to the hollow capstone of the pyramid. Begin your climb.

4 When you reach the interior of the large capstone, what appears as gold from outside on the ground, is actually totally transparent from inside. There is just room for you to move inside and sit on the stool in the exact centre.

5 To the east, the first blush of impending sunrise colours the horizon. To the west, a few bright stars are still visible in the inky black sky. As the light grows and spreads, the ribbon of the Nile below you becomes visible and soon the patchwork fields of the Nile valley come into view. To the west the sands of the desert begin to take on the golden glow of the eastern sky.

6 At the moment of sunrise, there is a surge of life force through you and throughout the world around you. It is the force that connects all levels of life. Feel your oneness with that force and with all you behold from your vantage point. Know that all life is One and you are part of that oneness. And, that there is a knowing, conscious purpose to all with which you are one. What is behind that purpose is formless, but is the source of all forms. It is the Great God.

7 When you feel a sense of completion with the process, take a few deep breaths, and become aware of your surroundings again. When you are ready, your eyes will open naturally.

Chapter 4
Gods and goddesses: mythology and the Goddess

It would be easy to dismiss the stories of Isis and Osiris, of Re and of Seth and of Nephtys as quaint fairytales. Yet to do so would be to miss an Egyptian treasure far more valuable than King Tut's tomb. For coded within these stories and others are some fundamental answers to modern life's problems. Only because we live in an age when the word 'myth' has come to mean 'lie' do we miss these vital messages from the past. The stories of mythology actually point the way to the spiritual life.

So what is it about myths? On the immediate level of life and structure, myths offer life models. Myths are archetypal dreams that deal with great human problems. They help us to know when we come to one of life's thresholds. The myth tells us about it and how to respond to it. The myths tell us where we are when we experience crises like disappointment or delight or failure or success. Further, myths contain truths about human beings and human life that are beyond expression in cold facts and figures. What myths and stories convey is beyond rational thought. That is why when the stories of mythology are translated into other languages and the figures cloaked in different costumes, they still have meaning in whatever culture they reappear. There are some good recent examples: the timeless Japanese story *The Seven Samurai* was dressed up in new costumes and became the classic western film *The Magnificent Seven*. The universal hero epic was loaded aboard spaceships and became *Star Wars*. They have universal appeal because they represent archetypal ideas, ideas fundamental to all human beings. And, indeed, the beingness of all humans.

Archetypes are biologically grounded, elementary ideas. All over the world and at different times of human history, these archetypes, or elementary ideas, have appeared in different forms depending on the environment and historical conditions. These archetypes are presented in the form of *metaphors*. A metaphor is an image that suggests something else. For instance, if we say to someone, 'You're really in a pickle', we're not suggesting that the person is actually inside a pickle. 'In a pickle' is a metaphor. The reference of the metaphor in religious traditions is to something so transcendent that it is literally not a 'thing'. When we speak of 'God' we are not talking about an actual person or thing – God is all things and forces beyond human understanding. Equally, religions that speak of the Goddess do not mean anything literal or physical. In the Goddess religions, the Goddess is a metaphor for Nature.

Two types of myth

The first type of myth are those metaphorical of the spiritual potential in the human being. The same powers that animate our own lives animate the life of the world. This is the mythology that relates you to your nature and to the natural world of which you are a part.

The second is the mythology that is strictly sociological, linking you to a particular society. You are not simply a natural person, you are a member of a particular group. Usually the socially oriented system is of a nomadic people who are moving around, so you learn that the group is where your centre is. A nature-oriented mythology is that of an earth-cultivating people, as in ancient Egypt.

Similarly in mythology, if you have a mythology in which the metaphor for life's mystery is the father, as is usually the case in nomadic peoples, you are going to have a different set of signals from that which you have if the metaphor for the wisdom and mystery of the world is the mother, as in earth-cultivating people. There is nothing wrong with either metaphor. Neither one is a fact; they are just metaphors.[1]

The functions of myths

Myth opens the door to the realization of the mystery that underlies all forms and even genders. It also shows us the shape of the universe in such a way that the mystery comes through. Myths can teach you how to live a human lifetime under any circumstances. What they deal with are exactly what all myths have dealt with – the maturation of the individual, from dependency through adulthood, through maturity and then to the world beyond.

The last function is in supporting and validating a certain social order. It is this sociological function of myth that has – unfortunately – taken over in our world. Myths become the laws of life as it should be in the 'good' society, forcing us to conform to society, to a certain social order, rather than our own inner nature.

Mythology and religion

A distinction must be made between mythology and religion. Religions all have their own mythological basis, but they are two very different versions of the same thing. Religion begins with the sense of wonder and awe and the attempt to tell stories that will connect us to God – our myths. Mythology is fluid. Many myths are even self-contradictory, giving different versions of the same mystery. Theology then says it can only be just one way. Then we are left with a set of theological works in which everything is reduced to a code, to a creed. Most religions are theology, not mythology. Mythology touches the broad essence – an essence lost when reduced to religious dogma. So, too, was the mythology of ancient Egypt reduced from a mythology in which the metaphors of the human condition were reduced to a set of theological creeds, rules and regulations. Joseph Campbell

---

[1] Campbell and Moyers, 1988.

described the process well: 'Religion turns poetry into prose. God is literally "up there", and this is literally what he thinks, and this is the way you've got to behave to get into proper relationship with that god up there.'

He also goes on to say: 'I think myth is coming back. There's a young scientist today who's using the term "morphogenetic field", the energy field that produces forms. That's who the Goddess is, the field that produces forms.' This is why we are looking back to the origins of Egyptian belief, before it degenerated into priestly dogmas and interpretations. When we understand the metaphor behind Egyptian religion, we see that it teaches us much about our own lives. There is much that has been lost to us in our modern, 'scientific', soulless view of the world.

Gods and goddesses

The word in the English language for that which is ultimate is 'God'. But the minute we give the ultimate a name, it becomes limited by its own definition; it becomes a concept for what is beyond concept. Campbell says: 'We project our idea of God onto the world. Our geography shapes our image of divinity, and then it is projected out and called God. The god idea is always culturally conditioned, always.' He points out that in a jungle, where there's no horizon and you never see anything more than 10 metres (30 feet) away, the idea of God is very different from what it would be if you lived out in the desert with one sky and one world. The idea of one God arose among desert people, whereas in the rainforest there have always been many gods.

'God' is an ambiguous word in our language anyway because it seems to refer to something that is known. God is transcendent, beyond names and forms. 'Transcendent' is a technical, philosophical term, usually translated in two different ways. In Christian theology, it materialistically refers to God as being beyond or outside the field of nature. God is thought of as a kind of spiritual 'being' existing somewhere 'out there'. Hegel spoke of our God as the 'gaseous vertebrate' – an idea of God that many Christians hold. Or, he is thought of as a temperamental, often petulant, bearded old man, given to being offended if we bow in the wrong direction or call him by the wrong name. But 'transcendent' properly means that which is beyond all concepts. All of our experiences are bounded by time and space – they take place within space and they take place in the course of time, except those rare experiences that are truly transcendent – the gasp of awe at a stunning sunset; the sudden overwhelming sense of wonder looking up at a sky full of stars; the sense of oneness with all when lying beneath a tree. Or, the moment of ultimate, profound revelation upon which all religions are based.

There are other ways of thinking about God, too. In the West we think of God as the father. In religions where the god is the mother, the whole world is her body. There is nowhere that is 'outside'. But the male god is usually somewhere 'out there'. Male and female are just two aspects of one principle, like up or down, left or right, positive or negative. When you substitute the male for the female, you get a different psychology, a different cultural bias.

You are born from your mother and your first experience is your mother. Your father may be absent, especially if you are born into a hunting culture, unknown to you, or he may be dead if you come from a warrior culture. Thus your mother is really a more immediate parent than your father.

In agricultural societies reverence was directed towards the Goddess figure, the Great Goddess, the mother earth. In the agricultural world of ancient Mesopotamia, Egypt, and in the earlier planting-culture systems the Goddess is predominant. Just as the human woman gives birth and nourishment, so too does the earth give birth and nourishment to the plants. The magic of the earth and the magic of the woman are the same. It is the female energy that gives birth to forms and nourishes forms.

The Great Goddess, mother of the universe and of us all, teaches us compassion for all living beings. You come to appreciate the sanctity of the earth itself, because it is the body of the Goddess. When you see the Goddess as the creator, it's her own body that is the universe. She is identical with the universe.

That's the sense of the Egyptian goddess Nut, who we meet in Chapter 5 – the whole sphere of the life-enclosing heavens. Spirit is not something breathed into life, it comes out of life.

The absent God

But when the God figure is a male, the whole concept changes. When Yahweh creates, he creates man from earth, but he does it from outside, he's not himself present in that form. Man was no longer an incarnation of divine life, but of a separate nature entirely, earthly and mortal. And the earth itself was now no longer part of the divine, but something separate. Matter and spirit had separated. Gods and humans were no longer both aspects of a single Being of beings. They were in nature distinct from each other, even opposed to each other – man is the sinner and God that which was sinned against, a meter-out of punishment. Humankind is now subordinate, required to pay due homage or face dire consequences.

But the Goddess is inside you as well as outside you. Your body is made of her body. You are quite literally one with the universe. Given all of this, it would seem that Goddess religions are much kinder and infinitely more desirable. But goddess religions are also out of balance when they only emphasize the feminine principle, as many did in the early days.

Historically the separation began in Mesopotamia in about 2000 BC, when a distinction began to be made between the king as a mere human being and the god whom he is now to serve. Unlike the pharaoh at the time, he is no longer a god-king; he is now the 'tenant farmer' of the god. His city becomes the god's earthly estate and the king is merely the chief steward or man in charge. The growth of the city-state was a prime factor in the new view of God. Since humans no longer lived among the gods, the gods came to live among humans. Now they lived in special god-houses: temples and churches. The same process was happening in Egypt, too, but it was a slower process. But when Egypt was conquered in 1780 BC, the injection of Mesopotamian ideas into Egyptian religion completed the process. God now became an 'idea', a thought, a construct of the brain, rather than an experience of the heart. Humans were no longer an incarnation of divine life, but of another nature entirely, earthly and mortal. This is why when we look for 'Goddess' wisdom in ancient Egypt, we must look well before this period.

But as we noted, the Goddess is not the be-all and end-all even so. Campbell reminds us: 'It is not easy for Westerners to realise that the ideas recently developed in the West of the individual, his selfhood, his rights, and his freedom, have no meanings whatsoever in the Orient. They had no meaning for primitive man.' They meant nothing to those living in early Mesopotamia, China, or India… or Egypt. There was no such thing as an individual life in cultures such as those. There is only one great cosmic law to which every individual must uncritically submit. Your birth determined what you were to be, as well as what you were to think and do. Even many European cultures operated on this basis until recently and many Eastern cultures still do.

Thus our quest is not for one or the other, but a balance of the two. In the West the pendulum has swung almost entirely to the male, impersonal god. The consequences have been dire, but a swing totally back to the female must, for the hard-won concept of the worth of the individual, be equally dire. There is no doubt that the Goddess must reappear if we are to survive on the earth, a lesson that the ancient Egyptians teach us well. In Chapter 8, The Return of the Goddess, we will look at how we can redress the balance, but for the moment we will look further at how we got to where we are, which holds clues to how we can get back to where we need to be.

Because ancient Egypt presents us with a concept of God generally at odds with the traditional Western concepts of God – indeed, to some Western minds it is a blasphemous concept – it is useful to sum up the Eastern and Western ideas. These ideas are essentially polarities, which are 'inclusive' and 'exclusive'. Eastern beliefs tend to be all-encompassing, a view of humankind as an integral part, but only a part, of the greater whole of the earth and cosmos. Western thought tends to exclude those not part of a specified belief system; Christian thought excludes all but Christians, Jewish thought all but Jews, etc.

As geography shapes our concept of God, so too is it suggested that the god idea is always culturally conditioned. I'm no so sure. I wonder if our culture isn't shaped by our image of God. Thus it becomes easy in the West to separate any and all thought: nature is separate from humans; God is separate from humans; we are separate from each other; spirit is separate from the material world; the ethics of business are separate from the ethics of personal interrelations, and so on. The East affirms the oneness of all things; the West denies it.

Yet the East generally fails to recognize that within the oneness of all things is virtually limitless opportunity for individual growth and development. We cannot transcend duality by ignoring it.

Your male or female gender is a springboard to launch you into the transcendent; to 'transcend' means to go past duality. You are born in only one aspect of your actual metaphysical duality. 'This is represented in the mystery religions, where an individual goes through a series of initiations opening him inside out into a deeper and deeper depth of himself, and there comes a moment when he realises that he is both mortal and immortal, both male and female.'[2]

The lost Goddess

Campbell also reminds us that the idea of the supernatural as being something over and above the natural is a killing idea. We still live in the residue of this idea today, an idea that became rooted in the Middle Ages. This was the idea that finally turned our world into something like a wasteland, a land where people live inauthentic lives, never doing a thing they truly want to because the supernatural laws require us to live as directed by our clergy. In a wasteland, people are fulfilling purposes that are not properly theirs but have been put upon them as inescapable laws. This has happened in those civilizations that have lost the Goddess. It happened in the ancient world when the shift took place from the personification of God from female to male.

---

[2] Campbell and Moyers, 1988.

It happened in Babylon. The Babylonians under Hammurabi went from a city to an empire in one generation and back to a city again in another generation or two, and within a few more generations, to a mound of brick rubble in the desert. It happened in Assyria. The Assyrians under Sennacherib and Assurbanipal rose from the city-state of Nineveh to envelop the Nile, hundreds of miles away; within a few generations, Nineveh went the way of Babylon. It happened in Greece. The Greeks under Philip II and Alexander went from a humble backwater in Macedonia to an empire reaching India; within a few years of Alexander's death it broke up into three bickering provinces. So, too, went the Roman and British Empires, and so, too, is the danger to all civilizations eventually who deny nature, who deny the Goddess.

And so, too, went the Egyptian civilization. As the Goddess principle weakened so too did Egypt. There was a renewal and an expansion in the New Kingdom, but it was a period of empire-building and failure to incorporate or assimilate conquered peoples. The Exodus took place during this period, which in itself serves as a metaphor for Egypt's failure of the Goddess. After a rapid peak there was a rapid decline, with Egypt being overrun by other, aggressive, male-god civilizations. By the time Egypt was definitely conquered by the Greeks in 330 BC, there was a little left that was purely Egyptian.

Perhaps, in a negative sense, this is one of the most important lessons we can draw from ancient Egypt.

Exercise

Meeting the Goddess

Pillow talk from ancient Egypt

This is an exercise designed to help you connect with the female dimension of the godhead. In the West, with our 'God the father' upbringings, most of us are conditioned to experience God as separate from ourselves, and ourselves separate from other people and things. When we begin to address god as 'mother', there is a subtle inner shift that increases our awareness of our oneness with all.

Here we are going to use the dream state as a point of contact. It is the time when our subconscious is nearer the surface and our conditioning is more able to be made visible.

There are two possible props for this exercise: first, get four poles – four garden bamboo poles about 2 metres (6 feet) long and 1 cm (half an inch) or so in diameter will do nicely – and attach them to the corners of your bed in a pyramid shape. If this is impractical, a small glass or crystal pyramid can be placed beneath your pillow.

As you go to sleep, visualize the Goddess overlighting your bed and your dreams, and ask to be shown something to bring you closer to Goddess-awareness within yourself. Remember that what you are really invoking is a closer connection to the natural world of which you are a part.

In your awake state, be aware of the times you think of, or speak to, God. If you are from a God-The-Father background, start to address your thoughts and prayers first to 'Father', and then the same thoughts or prayers to 'Mother'. Be aware of your own responses first of all and then of the response of the world to those thoughts or prayers.

Chapter 5
Isis and the Goddess principle

Egyptian creation stories all begin with the sun god Re. There are various depictions of Re, influenced in no small part by changes in the political climate of Egypt. Re, as the primary state god, was essentially connected with 'divinity' of the pharaohs, and as the position and influence of the pharaoh changed, so too, conveniently, did Re. But his classical representation gives us insight into the earliest Egyptian understanding of their world. As the sun at dawn, he is depicted as a beetle (Khepri), or a beetle-headed man. But the Egyptian word *khepri* was derived from the word *kheper*, meaning 'to become or exist'. Thus the subtle message is that the rising sun, Re, is both the rising sun and the self-existent creator of the universe. The lowering sun was depicted as an aged, wise old man of good counsel, conveying also a sense of 'completion'.

There are numerous variations on the theme of the solar cycle, but it is unnecessary to list them. In every case, the cycle itself is the constant meaning, both the daytime portion of birth, ageing and completion, and the night-time portion of regeneration.

Various stories surround Re's creation of the world, but one of the most widespread was his appearance from watery chaos on a mound, from where he proceeds to create a pair of deities – Shu and Tefenet who, in turn, create Geb and Nut, the earth and the sky. Their children were Isis and Osiris, and Seth and Nephtys. Once again, there are numerous local variations, but throughout them is a consistent mythological thread: that there is an idea of death to the past and birth to the future in our lives and our thinking; death to the animal nature and birth to the spiritual. And, although you can have rebirth through the male, using the Egyptian system of symbols the woman becomes the regenerator.

The Isis and Osiris story

Isis and her husband Osiris were twins, born from the goddess Nut, from Mother Nature. Their younger brother and sister, Seth and Nephtys, were also twins, born likewise from Nut.[1] One night Osiris mistakenly made love to Nephtys, thinking she was Isis. From that mistaken union, Osiris' oldest son, Anubis, was born.

Nephtys' husband Seth wasn't at all pleased with this event and planned to kill his older brother, Osiris. He had a beautiful sarcophagus (ornate coffin) made just to Osiris' measurements, which had been secretly taken. When the Gods were together celebrating, Seth offered the sarcophagus as a gift to whoever it fitted perfectly. All of the gods tried and, of course, it fitted Osiris exactly. But when Osiris was lying in it, 72 accomplices of Seth rushed out and slammed the lid on. They fastened it down and dragged it to the Nile, where they cast it in.

The death of Osiris was symbolically associated with the annual inundation of the Nile, the event which restores Egypt's fertility and hence its civilization and wealth. It is as if Osiris' decomposing body revitalized the land each year.

In the story, Osiris' sarcophagus floated down the Nile and was washed up on a beach in faraway Syria. A majestic tree with sweet-smelling flowers grew up around the sarcophagus, which

---

[1] The native Americans from the north-east woods also told of a woman who fell from the sky and gave birth to twins. The native Americans of the south-west told a story of twins born to a virgin mother. There are many examples in other cultures, but this serves to demonstrate the universality of the images.

became embedded in its trunk. Now the Syrian king had a newborn son and was about to build a new palace. So he had the tree cut down to become the central pillar of the great hall of the new palace.

Isis, in the meanwhile, had begun a search for her husband's body. A theme runs through the various creation myths of the period, both in Egyptian and other cultures: the Goddess who goes in search of her lost spouse or lover. Through her sacrifice and descent into the world of the dead, she lifts him back into the world of life. She becomes his deliverer. Thus Isis eventually comes to Syria and learns of the new palace, with its majestic and fragrant pillar. Suspecting a connection to Osiris, she becomes nurse to the new-born child. She loves the child and decides in her role as Goddess to grant him immortality. She does this by placing him in the fireplace to burn away his mortal body, but as a goddess she can prevent the fire from killing him. She does this each day, in the evening. And while the child is in the fire, she transforms herself into a swallow, to mournfully circle the column where Osiris lies. The flying bird is a universal figure representing the spirit. It is later represented in Egyptian symbolism as a human-headed bird, which is the ka, the spirit.

While all of this is going on one evening, the Queen, the child's mother, walks into the room. She sees her son in the fireplace and lets out a scream. This breaks the spell and the child has to be rescued from being burned. As the spell breaks, the swallow is transformed back into Isis, who has some explaining to do! She tells the whole story to the Queen and to the King who has now arrived. She also explains that the sarcophagus in the column contains the body of her husband, and asks if she could have him back. The King agrees at once and has the column removed. The sarcophagus is then extracted and is taken back to the Nile on a royal barge. While on the journey up the Nile, Isis removes the lid of the sarcophagus, lies upon the dead Osiris and conceives — he is a god, after all! When the barge comes to land in a papyrus swamp, Isis gives birth to Horus. This is Osiris' last earthly act, whereupon he descends to become ruler of the underworld, the Egyptian equivalent of 'heaven'. It is, in effect, the prototype ascension story.

As Joseph Campbell points out, this is a common theme running through the mythology of all cultures: *out of death comes life*. In Egyptian symbolism, Isis represents the throne and the child Horus on her lap is the pharaoh. Thus every pharaoh is the child of Isis, the Great Mother, the Goddess, the source of all Egyptian civilization. It is also the symbol of the Divine Mother that became the model for the Madonna.

Isis then becomes the exemplary mother, raising Horus to manhood. As he is brought to manhood, Isis brings about the victory of Horus over venomous animals: he is stung by a scorpion and is restored to health with the aid of Re and Thoth. In Egyptian medicine, Isis becomes the deity to be invoked, with the patient in the role of Horus. Horus gains protective and curative powers in his own right and becomes a saviour figure.

Seth, Osiris' younger brother, had meanwhile usurped the throne. As Horus reaches manhood, he takes the title of avenger of his father. Horus contests the throne with Seth for many years and eventually they fight a great battle in which both are maimed. Horus' eye is torn out and is magically restored by Thoth. The restored eye, The Eye of Horus, became the most powerful magical symbol and was frequently worn as an amulet. In the end, although defeated by Horus, Seth was retained and even honoured as a god, becoming the necessary personification of disorder, evil and destruction. In this respect, he is much like the Hindu god Shiva, the destroyer. It is an acknowledgement that destruction of the old is an essential part of the rebirth of the new.

Osiris

Because he was connected with the most basic mysteries of life – death and resurrection – Osiris was the most significant of male Egyptian gods. Osiris may well claim to be the longest-worshipped god in the world. From the beginning of Egyptian civilization until the eradication of his cult by Christians in the fourth century AD, he was the primary god of the Egyptian pantheon. The earliest written records, the Pyramid Texts of about 2500 BC are full of him, mainly in his role in the afterworld of the pharaoh. Early stories about him vary, but are concerned to various degrees with his relationship to other gods and goddesses of his time, and his death and resurrection. He is always depicted wrapped in mummy bandages, but with protruding hands holding the crook and flail, the emblems of kingship. Although he was returned to life, he did not continue his life on earth, but became lord of the underworld.

Another connected tradition was the death of Isis, who was not deified until after her death. Parts of her body were supposedly sent to different temple centres. Both this story and the Osiris story offer an intriguing question: Were Isis and Osiris real people, possibly from the group of lawgivers and civilizers remembered as bringing civilization to other groups like the Tibetans, the Mayans and the Mesopotamians? Whereas in the other cultures the lawgivers were remembered as such, is it possible that in Egypt they were remembered as gods?

We do know one thing for certain: many powerful images and beliefs are centred around Isis and Osiris. The Christian image of Madonna and Child is borrowed directly from the classic Egyptian image of Isis with the infant Horus on her lap (the early churchmen said so themselves) and the death and resurrection story of Christ is a virtual copy of the Osiris story. And for the believers, both Egyptian and Christian, both of these stories offered the hope of eternal life and resurrection to humans.

There is one other significant dimension to the Osiris story: the dead person being presented to Osiris after The Weighing of the Heart actually *becomes* Osiris or *an* Osiris if his or her heart is pure. Their name after death becomes 'the Osiris...' followed by his or her name. Thus the pure become one with their god. This, of course, is anathema and a virtual blasphemy to Western beliefs, where the god is a distant god, to be emulated but never equalled. But in Eastern thought, where a person is part of the oneness of all creation, you are one with God anyway. The only thing which sets you apart is your own failure to live in harmony with the flow of life around you, the Ma'at. So to become 'an Osiris' means to become what you already are, but are separated from because you have failed to live in the harmony of Ma'at.

The messages of the Isis—Osiris story

Aside from the elements discussed above there are, within the Isis—Osiris story, a number of key elements to the understanding not only of Egyptian wisdom and belief, but of restoring those same lost attributes to modern life.

The first understanding is to read the word 'nature' for 'goddess'. As we have discovered, in mythological terms they are virtually the same. In the Isis story, we have the Goddess Isis, nature, in search of her lost lover — natural man, Osiris. He has become lost through his mistake, embracing Isis's twin. But when we realize that in mythology the twin takes the opposition polarity, Isis's twin then becomes the spiritual opposite of Isis, the opposite of nature. Thus, natural man has strayed from nature through his own ignorance and reaps the consequences by his loss of 'aliveness'. In the end he must be reborn and, as Horus, must contest with the opposite side of his own nature — represented by Seth — to reattain rightness.

Although Osiris' body is decomposing in a faraway place, Isis seeks him out and finds him. Even though decomposing, his body gives off a sweet aroma — the essence of his eternal self. This essence becomes the very pillar of the womb of new life — the king's palace, wherein the new-born is nurtured. Nature herself becomes the servant of the new infant and puts him through a purifying process — sitting him in the fire. Isis, as nature, then becomes a spirit, symbolized by the swallow, circling and connecting with the essence of Osiris, the lost truth of naturalness. In the fire all that is not natural burns away. It is a standard mythological metaphor for the process of spiritual growth and unfoldment.

When the spell is broken, the king, as the action principle, releases the body of Osiris. On the way back to Egypt, Isis is impregnated with the truth of Osiris, the truth of 'natural man', and returns to Egypt carrying that truth in the form of the infant Horus. Horus is represented in Egyptian iconography as either a hawk-headed man or just as a hawk. The hawk soars above all that is coarse and unnatural, and is closest to the sun, the giver of life to all.

Thus Isis, nature, descends into the world of the dead, the world where aliveness is diminished through loss of 'naturalness,' to return with renewed life on a higher plane. It is a story that could well be set in the late twentieth century.

There is a second reading of the story as well. It has been speculated that the Egyptian, as well as several other ancient civilizations, arose from a yet older civilization that disappeared, and that teachers and the wise from that older civilization spread into the world to pass on their wisdom to still-emerging civilizations. It could well be that the Isis–Osiris story records that as well. The old civilization may have been 'impregnated' with the wrong knowledge that led to its collapse, and Isis carried 'within' her the grain of truth from which Egypt arose.

The status of women in ancient Egypt

From this account of the Goddess, an obvious question arises: What is the role of women in goddess cultures? Historically, women have not fared too well in ancient cultures. But a further examination of history will show that as the culture shifted from a female to a male god-metaphor, the position of women declined accordingly. In purely goddess cultures, the opposite was untrue for men, principally because of the all-inclusive nature of goddess-thought. This is another important lesson from ancient Egypt: men have nothing to fear from nature or goddess religions and cultures.

In ancient Egypt women had a legal status only slightly below men: they could own and sell property and could initiate legal proceedings and divorce in their own right. Thus divorce was more akin to modern Western divorce, where the woman's rights to joint property are equal to her husband's. Women rarely held administrative office but dominated many religious cults as priestesses or 'chantresses'. High-status married women were often given the title 'mistress of the house', although precisely what the title meant is not known. Lower-class women were as likely as their men to work in the fields as well as in the house. In tomb decoration, women's skins are usually portrayed with a yellowish-hue, while men's are red-brown. This suggests that women of a status high enough to afford tomb decoration generally had less exposure to the sun and were more concerned with indoor, domestic tasks as, indeed, one might expect. However, this does not necessarily imply a lower status for women, as the same skin-tone is used in pictures of high-status male bureaucrats, who, presumably, mostly worked indoors.

There is indirect evidence that women had considerable freedom of movement. An inscription of Ramses III states: 'I enabled the woman of Egypt to go her way, her journeys being extended where she wanted, without any other person assaulting her on the road.' Clearly there were other problems at the time with women travelling, but it may also be implied that were she travelling in the company of men, she would have had little fear of assault. Hence, the travel of women by themselves must have been commonplace enough that its increased safety would rate a royal boast.

Given the antiquity of Egyptian civilization and the status of women in comparable civilizations elsewhere in the East, even those with Goddess religions, Egypt was remarkably enlightened in its treatment of women.

Marriage

Egyptians were generally monogamous, with the nuclear family as the ideal. There is no known formal or legal ceremony or sanction for marriage, although it would be surprising if one did not exist, as every culture known formalizes marriage commitment in one form or another. Evidence does exist for the status of people living together, which was different from a married couple. That such an arrangement was formally recognized is in the record of a man being charged with having intercourse with a woman who was living with another man. Clearly the shared living situation was of sufficient legal status that its violation was a legal offence. Marriage to one's close blood relatives was virtually unknown although it was theoretically possible, except among the royal family, where brother–sister marriages are sometimes recorded. Divorce was easy but costly.

Sexuality

In Goddess religions generally, sexuality is regarded as natural and everyday, and therefore there is little worth writing down about it. So it appears to be early in Egyptian life, before the male-god influences of Asia became part of Egyptian religion. Sexual motifs and related inscriptions are rare in early Egyptian tombs. Sexuality was regarded as sacred because of its connection to creation and was also associated with rebirth in the hereafter. In an early tomb at Saqqara, the owner of the tomb and his wife are shown sitting on a bed facing each other while she plays the harp for him. This loving scene is as near to an erotic scene as appears early in Egyptian history.

Another early reference to sexuality is in *The Book of the Dead*. Osiris is complaining to Atum that there is 'no sexual gratification here'. Atum tells him 'I have given transfiguration in the place of water, air, and gratification, and peace of heart in place of bread and beer.' The Book does not record Osiris' response!

Women and sexuality in the New Kingdom

The New Kingdom, the period when the male-god influences from the Asian conquests of Egypt were becoming entrenched, may be singled out as a low point in the status of women. During this period women are increasingly portrayed both as male fantasy figures and the seducers and debasers of men. The evil seductress becomes a common theme and romantic poetry is written in the words of a woman filled with desire. Stories of seduction, both male and female, appear more generally, and erotic scenes are more common both in inscriptions and on papyri. Long hair was apparently eroticized, and in these scenes women are shown either with very long hair, or with heavy wigs. Indeed, in one New Kingdom story the evil seductress targets her husband's brother, accusing him of saying to her: 'Come, let us spend an hour lying together. Put on your wig.'

The New Kingdom is also dubiously notable for producing the only obscene document of any size. In it, a series of sexual encounters are shown between a corpulent man and a woman or a series of women. The woman is dressed in jewellery, a belt and a wig. The papyrus also has scenes of animals acting out human sexual roles, suggesting that the sexual act had its humorous side for ancient Egyptians.

It is likewise in the New Kingdom that clay figures, both of men and of women, begin to appear in larger numbers. Both male and female figures have outsized genitalia. Such figures appeared much earlier in Mesopotamia, as the goddess figures there became tools of the male-oriented society. It is possible that these are erotic objects, but it is perhaps more likely that they are fertility objects. Most of them, especially the female figures, are rather crude and have a hand-made appearance, suggesting they were made by peasant women seeking increased fertility. The New Kingdom was a time when ritual magic dominated religious practice, as the Goddess connection became more tenuous.

One important conclusion to be drawn from ancient Egypt is the connection between the male-god image and the lowered status of women. European history from the Middle Ages onward bears that out with distressing accuracy. Again, the desired effect is not to discard the male-image for the female, but to find the healthy balance between the two. As the Isis and Osiris story tells us, to abandon nature and human naturalness is a kind of death. A death that only the restoration of the feminine principle can resurrect.

Visualization

Finding the barriers to the natural you

This is a long meditation, but it is a major one that can be used time and time again to uncover increasingly subtle blockages that keep us separated from the source of our being. You may not go all the way to the top of the pyramid each time – just do what feels right for you. But however high you go, always come down in the reverse order of the chambers.

This meditation uses the inner sanctum of the pyramid as a metaphor for the deepest inner self, where all blockages become visible.

1 Close your eyes and find yourself standing at the head of the avenue of sphinxes, leading to the entrance of a pyramid.

2 When you are ready, the moment has come to start your journey.

3 You reach the ramp leading up into the pyramid and you enter. The corridor into the centre of the pyramid is lit with torches and, as you enter, the cool stone surrounds you. As you walk further inwards, you reach the doorway to the lowest chamber and enter. It is lit by a single red-burning candle, bathing the chamber in soft red light. In the wall opposite is the door to a climbing passageway to the chamber above. Against the wall to your right is a gilded chair. Be seated in the chair and relax.

4 In the wall opposite the chair is another doorway. From this doorway will emerge a red figure that is you, your ka. This red ka will show you where certain of your inner barriers are, and may have something to tell you or show you about yourself and some suggestions about how to begin dismantling the barriers at the red level of your being.

5 When it has done all that is necessary, it will depart. Make a clear intention to remember what it has shown you, then rise and turn to the doorway on your right. Climb upwards to the next chamber, lit with an orange-burning candle. The orange chamber is laid out exactly like the red chamber, again with the door to the chamber above in the wall opposite you.

6 Be seated as before and, as before, your orange ka will appear. Again there will be something shown to you about yourself. When it has done all that is necessary, it will depart. Make a clear intention to remember what it has shown you, then rise and turn to the doorway on your right. Climb upwards to the next chamber, lit with a yellow-burning candle.

7 The yellow chamber is laid out exactly like the previous chambers and, again, your yellow ka will appear and impart information as before. When you are complete with your yellow ka, climb to the next chamber above, the green chamber, in the exact centre of the pyramid, where your green ka will appear.

8 Complete with your green ka as before, and then your blue, indigo and purple chambers and kas, in that order.

9 When you have completed your purple chamber, there is one left to go, the chamber right in the very capstone of the pyramid. This chamber is lit only dimly, with a very soft, crystal-clear glow that seems to come from the stones themselves. Be seated in the chair to your right. Very slowly, just enough for comfort, the light will begin to increase. When your eyes are comfortable and adjusted, from the doorway opposite will come your universal ka, your ka that is one with the whole of creation. It is transparent, made of clear, brilliant light, the light from which all the other kas come. It, too, will have something to show you about yourself.

10 When you are complete with your universal ka, it too will exit. When it has gone, begin to descend the way you came up, first to the purple chamber, then to the indigo, blue, green and so on back down to the red chamber.

11 When you are ready, take a few deep breaths, step out of the pyramid into the sunshine and become aware of your surroundings again. When you are ready, your eyes will open naturally.

Chapter 6
The rhythms of the Nile

One of the highest wisdoms of the ancient Egyptians was their absolute understanding of the rhythms and cycles of nature, and the need for human life to live in harmony with and as part of those cycles and rhythms. They knew that rhythms and cycles are fundamental to all life; indeed, it might be said that they are life itself. As you begin to open yourself and your heart to your own deep inner self-awareness, you will begin to sensitize yourself not only to your own natural rhythms, but to the rhythms of the world around you. Opening the heart is indirectly the subject of Chapter 7, but let us now look at some of the rhythms to which it is superbly attuned when it is open.

Rhythms connected to health and well-being

Rhythms related to our biology are the major group of rhythms which align us with the world around us. Some of these factors affect the brain directly (such as shifts in the geomagnetic field), while some rhythms are part of the larger rhythm of cosmic movements. One thing of which we are all aware, whether we recognize its source or not, is that our sense of pleasure in life is disturbed by any upset to our own natural rhythms. Psychiatrist Alexander Lowen defines pleasure as '…the conscious perception of the rhythmic and pulsatory activity of the body'. He further states:

The feeling of pleasure that stems from a natural and undisturbed rhythm of life embraces all our activities and relationships. There is a time to work and a time to rest, a time to play and a time to be serious, a time to be together and a time to be alone. Too much togetherness can be as painful as too much aloneness, and too much play can be as dull as too much work. The rhythms that govern life are inherent in life; they cannot be imposed from without. Each individual knows what his rhythms are and knows by the feelings of pain or lack of pleasure when his rhythms are disturbed.[1]

That these rhythms have correlations to the larger rhythms of the earth and the cosmos is hardly surprising. The earth itself moves to a larger set of patterns, and life that evolved on the earth must, of necessity, evolve from those same rhythms. Survival could hardly dictate otherwise.

For example, in the 1980s, a new field appeared called psychoneuroimmunology, which recognizes that the immune system, far from being merely a reactor to the presence of pathogens like viruses, is fully communicative and interactive with other organs and, in particular, with the hormonal and nervous systems. The interactions, in fact, go in both directions. The brain influences the immune system and the antibodies produced by the immune system influence the brain. Antibodies, for example, influence the firing rates of brain neurones and stress causes the portion of the brain called the hypothalamus to trigger the pituitary gland to produce the hormone ACTH which, in turn, triggers the production of other hormones which suppress the response of the immune system – which in turn influences the brain through its reduced production of antibodies. The general effects of stress on the immune system are well known, but the amount of stress generated by lifestyle is not yet fully recognised. The person living an arrhythmic lifestyle puts his or her immune system under constant pressure and the mental state is affected as part of a vicious circle that eventually can lead to some from of physical or mental breakdown. That such lifestyles are considered 'normal' in our culture is scarcely recognized as a contributing factor to the high level of physical and mental illness

---

[1] Lowen, p.236.

that surrounds us. One medical investigator even goes so far as to suggest that 'the immune system serves as a sensory organ for those stimuli not recognised by the classic sensory system.'[2] The classic example of such 'stimuli' are the disturbances and stresses generated by living out of harmony with the natural world.

As modern humans have moved into cities and fewer people inhabit the countryside, our culture has, to a large extent, lost contact with the natural world around us. The electric light has negated the day–night cycle, central heating has obliterated winter and the supermarket has replaced the harvest. Even worse, the noise and pollution and electronic jumble of the city has dulled our exquisite sensitivities to the subtle rhythms of nature. It is more than a sad loss. It just may possibly, in the end, prove fatal.

Organic life is absolutely dependent on and regulated by rhythm – the basic processes of individual cells, their constituent atoms and molecules, individual body organs of animals, the functioning of the various components that make up plants – exactly the same rhythms that govern minutely the functioning of our own bodies, minds and spirits.

That humans routinely ignore or even dismiss the existence of such rhythms within themselves distances us from one of our most highly evolved survival mechanisms. Maintaining rhythm is absolutely essential to the survival of all organisms. Loss of rhythm in one part of an organism which is not quickly regained can upset the life process of the entire organism. Experiments with insects and with lower animals have shown that artificially imposed rhythms, de-synchronization with natural rhythm, is frequently fatal: a message that we can scarcely afford to ignore.

All things in the universe move in rhythms and cycles and patterns: the changing seasons, the movement of planets, the birth and death of stars, your own changing insights into who you really are. Polarity is also a rhythm: positive and negative, light and dark, male and female, good and bad, and so on.

Our own everyday lives move in a number of patterns and rhythms. Some are biological, some are psychological and some

---

[2] Balcock, 1984.

are developmental – each cycle leading us further along the path to self-realization. The psychological and developmental cycles are often the most difficult, requiring us at each stage to confront our fears and insecurities. It is all part of the rhythms of growth, common to both humans and the universe. Rhythm is the connecting thread that weaves all levels of life into one.

The rhythms of time

Rhythms and cycles and patterns themselves are interconnected by a common denominator: they are all a product of time. The Egyptians understood time very well. The Egyptian year began with the rising of the star Sirius above the horizon, several weeks before the annual inundation of the Nile began. The calendar was lunar and very accurate. The year was 365 days, with an extra day added every fourth year. The Egyptians were not only acutely aware of time in the general, linear sense – one year follows another – but they knew that time is also circular.

There are cycles and rhythms that are a vital part of human life – patterns of psychological and spiritual growth and development that are less well defined in a 'scientific' sense and yet no less noticeable in our own lives. One reason that they remain largely unknown is that they are connected to our Western concept of time. We view time as strictly linear – past, present, future. When the present is past, we are finished with it; it is over, never to be repeated. We seldom notice that the present is an outgrowth of, and a direct result of, all the accumulated pasts. The past is always part of the present. We even have a saying about this: 'Those who fail to learn from the lessons of history are doomed to repeat them'. Because we see the present as disconnected from the past, we never mentally connect the two – and almost inevitably have to repeat the lessons.

Like the ancient Egyptians, most modern Eastern cultures still view time as circular – a progression of seasons and life-phases drawing to a natural conclusion to evolve into the next cycle in which the lessons of the previous cycle are repeated, except at a higher level of growth, depending on what has been learned in the previous cycle. If we are growing and evolving, all that changes in the next cycle is our perception of events and our response to them; yet our life is tied inseparably to those events through our past experience and past responses to them. It is a view that bears more resemblance to the realities of nature and to human development than does linear time.

It is not a requirement of this book that the reader accept such a view – cycles and rhythms occur no matter how we interpret the time-frame in which they occur.

Most cultures that recognize the circle as the fundamental structure of the universe have tended to put themselves at the centre of it. China used to call itself the Kingdom of the Centre, as did the Aztecs. The famous Aztec Calendar Stone is a great circle, reflecting a belief in circular time. The Egyptians had a similar belief, but because Egypt is long and narrow, the circle got flattened out quite a bit. In the images of Nut, the mother goddess of the sky, we see her arching across from horizon to horizon, with the earth itself completing the circle. In other images, Re, the sun god, travels across the sky in his boat during the day and completes the circle as he travels through the underworld during the night.

The circle, too, is the origin of the idea of burial, for rebirth. You put someone back into the womb of mother earth to be reborn. Very early images of the earth goddess, both in Egypt and elsewhere, show her as a mother receiving the soul back again.

The ancient Egyptians also understood *eternity*. They understood that eternity has nothing to do with time. Eternity isn't some later time. Eternity isn't even a long time. When the heart was weighed and Thoth looked at how you used the gifts of your lifetime, one of the gifts was *time*, and one of the qualities that showed how you used the gift of time was how much you experienced that which was *eternal*. Eternity is a dimension of here and now that you loose when you start thinking purely in terms of time. It is a *quality of being*, and if you don't get it here, you won't get it anywhere. But the experience of eternity right here and now, in all things, whether thought of as good or as evil, is the function of life.

Earth rhythms

Many of life's rhythms correspond with astronomical rhythms. Scientists have long believed that the governing factors of *all* rhythms are simple and obvious: the intensity of sunlight or moonlight, or their absence; the strength of tides or the temperature or the humidity. These have been found to be the controllers of many rhythms. Zoologist John Palmer tells us that:

> *Rhythms that match the geophysical periods of the earth... are ubiquitous in their distribution throughout the living kingdoms. It is thought this clock capability arose long ago in some primitive organism, where it was found to have a significant survival ability in that it could 'notify' its owner in advance of coming periodic environmental events, such as sunrise, sunset, and the flood tide.*[3]

Indeed, many of the rhythmic body cycles may be linked in just such a manner to external cosmic rhythms. Recent studies have shown, for example, that the menstrual cycle is much closer to the 29.5-day lunar month than to the 28-day cycle usually given. Ovulation occurs closer to day 15 than to day 14. The effect of the moon on human behaviour has been noted since ancient times. The word 'lunatic' was coined by the Romans and was applied in describing epileptics, who were observed to have more seizures than usual at the time of the full moon. In the sixteenth century, Paracelsus claimed that 'the insane grew worse at the dark of the moon' when the moon's attraction on the brain was believed to be the strongest. Such beliefs were legalized in eighteenth-century England, at which time a distinction was made between the 'insane', which designated the chronically and hopelessly psychotic, and 'lunatic' aberrations which were believed to be accelerated only by the full moon. Prior to 1808 Bedlam Hospital inmates were beaten at certain lunar periods as a 'prophylaxis against violence'.

Dr Arnold Lieber, author of *The Lunar Effect*, believes that the moon has an unbalancing effect on our body fluids and body chemistry as well as our body's electromagnetic field. In a reasonably well-balanced person this has an unsettling effect

---

[3] Palmer, pp.23–4.

resulting in restlessness or discomfort, but in those with biochemical imbalances leading to violent behaviour, it is enough to push them over the edge. As an example, manic-depressives who exhibit maniacal behaviour at the full moon are found to have an accelerated metabolism during the full-moon time – accelerated to the point where beard growth is greater.

The findings of Dr R. J. Ravitz support the contentions of Dr Lieber: for years Dr Ravitz has been measuring the differences in electrical potential between the head and chest of mental patients, which were found to change from day to day. He found that even in normal people there are cyclical changes from day to day, cycles which parallel seasonal and lunar changes. In the autumn and winter he found that maximum positivity occurs around the time of the new moon, and maximum negativity around the time of the full moon. He found that in mental patients, the difference in potential is markedly greater. But he does not take this to mean that the moon affects people directly; rather, that its position modifies the Earth's electromagnetic field, to which humans have a known sensitivity. In a person whose mental balance is precarious, it is enough to precipitate behaviour changes.[4] It is another sample of how human life is in continuous interchange and interaction with all that surrounds us.

This, too, underlines why when humans try to live lifestyles that ignore or oppose their own natural rhythms, health may suffer. We are exquisitely sensitive to natural forces. Our bodies are finely tuned to them; they evolved in specific response to natural rhythms. We sometimes forget that the human species is like any other form of animal life: it has evolved to fill a specific biological and temporal niche. When we violate the conditions set on us by our own evolution we are going against the very conditions which preserve us as a species. It is a lesson we can scarcely afford to forget.

An example of how health suffers when our cycles are out of rhythm is in the development of depression. Studies in the United Kingdom have shown a strong correlation between depression and disrupted circadian – daily – rhythms. Depression

---

[4] Dr L. J. Ravitz, quoted in Gauquelin, 1969.

resulting from disrupted rhythm is not merely a mood disturbance, 'the blues' (although there *are* rhythms to mood). Rather, it involves an upset of a number of cyclic body rhythms including those that regulate sleep, eating, concentration, memory and motivation.[5] These are all affected by depression and all have their own separate but co-ordinated cycles.

A more recently recognised cyclic depression is Seasonal Affective Disorder (SAD). In other species, migration or hibernation is triggered by the length of the day, and studies in humans are seeking a similar mechanism which may connect it to SAD. One neurotransmitter implicated is serotonin, which has marked seasonal rhythm in humans.

In a textbook devoted to the study of childhood disease and circadian disruption, Rolf Zurbrugg of the Department of Paediatrics at the University of Bern states: 'The structure of time is probably the most overlooked dimension of human life, both in health and disease. The importance of human rhythmicity for medical diagnosis and therapy is not yet generally recognised.'[6]

Dr Zurbrugg's studies of infants correlate well with other studies of adults: that the disruption of circadian rhythms causes disrupted hormone concentrations (which also have their own natural rhythms), which in turn leads to disruption of other body systems such as those mentioned above that are dependent on hormone levels. In particular, oxytocin and cortisol have been shown to be particularly dependent on maintenance of rhythm. Both are critical in memory, motivation and mood regulation.

But beyond these, it has also been shown that circadian disruption leads to immune-system abnormalities, even to the point of being implicated in tumour development.[7]

Other rhythmic sensitivities in humans which are related to health are those to allergens, alcohol and drugs. In several tests with different allergens (such as household dust and penicillin), the most violent reactions occurred around 11 p.m. and the least violent around 11 am. While these findings are interesting in

---

[5] Healy and Williams, pp.163–78.
[6] Zurbrugg, p.12.
[7] Healy and Williams, pp.169.

themselves, what they point to is even more important from the health standpoint – the body has a rhythmic sensitivity to drugs. It has been found that drugs are more effective and the effects last longer when administered in the morning (around 7 am) than when administered 12 hours later.[8] Thus morning doses need to be smaller than evening doses to gain the same effect. Equally, the safe dosage is much smaller in the morning than in the evening because its effects are greater.

There are longer-term rhythms as well – the so-called biorhythms. There is evidence for a 23-day physical cycle, a 28-day emotional cycle and a 33-day intellectual cycle. The idea of biorhythms has been dismissed to a degree in later years, but it must be remembered that a person living an arrhythmic lifestyle as most of us do in the Western world will tend to upset *all* of our natural rhythms, making many of them less susceptible to analysis. But in other quarters the subject is taken seriously: Japan Air Lines, for example, is one of several airlines that refuses to let its pilots fly on their 'down' days.

In plants collected for medicinal purposes, it has been noticed that their potencies are constantly changing, often in relationship to the phases of the moon. A cancer research institute in Switzerland found in its study of mistletoe 'that the properties of the plant were drastically affected not only by the local time and weather conditions, but by... the phases of the moon and the occurrence of an eclipse.'[9] The Druids 2,000 years ago ascribed medicinal properties to mistletoe, which were believed to vary with the phase of the moon in which the mistletoe was cut. In Egyptian medicine 2,000 years before the Druids, plant remedies were numerous and there was a similar awareness – texts speak of the 'harvest season' for medicinal plants. Additionally, there were certain plants that required gathering at certain times of the day. Where the active drug in the plant in question was an alkaloid – for example, morphine – there is a definite daily variation in its concentration. That the Egyptians understood such variations illustrates their acute awareness of the cycles and rhythms of nature, and the need to accommodate them in daily life.

[8] Palmer, pp.155–7.
[9] Whitman, p.134.

The fully realized human is totally at one with his or her 'animal' nature, the nature fully in harmony with the ebb and flow of the natural rhythms of the world. Indeed, we would not be fully human if we did *not*. Beyond that, a person not fully at one with that nature becomes ill as a consequence, either physically or mentally. There is an ongoing sense of unease with one's self, a continuing sense of something lacking in one's life. In our society we attempt to fill that lack with goods, or with 'success', or with 'winning'. But what we are really missing is the connection to an essential part of ourselves, the part of us that exists as an integral part of the natural environment. Without it we miss essential cues to our own growth and our development as fully realized human beings becomes side-tracked.

There is another reason for rhythm and cycle: growth. Gail Sheehy describes the process:

> *We are not unlike a particularly hardy crustacean. The lobster grows by developing and shedding a series of hard, protective shells. Each time it expands from within, the confining shells must be sloughed off. It is left exposed and vulnerable until, in time, a new covering grows to replace the old.*[10]

Growth always means moving through barriers – physical, mental, emotional and spiritual. This requires energy; energy creates tension; tension propels us through the barriers to growth. The build-up of tension and its release, a cyclic process, is the basis of growth.

Exercises

Reconnecting to nature is a practical experience. Visualizations are powerful tools, but *doing* also has its place. Here are two exercises for that purpose. As we open ourselves to deeper levels of our own Being, we also begin attuning ourselves to our own natural pulse of life. In doing so, we likewise begin to become aware of the pulse of all life around us. Many of you already have a high attunement to nature; it is perhaps through this attunement that many of you began to

---

[10] Sheehy, p.29.

realize that your own life exists beyond the boundaries of your physical body.

Exercise 1

Earlier in this chapter we discussed circular time, the cycles and rhythms and patterns of nature. To see the cycles and patterns in your own life, you need to make three lists: Relationships, Career and Money. Under each, write down in date order significant events or turning points in each. Under Relationships, write down all of your past and present relationships, and the pattern of their development. Under Career, list each job you got, and the jobs you wanted and didn't get. For each job in both categories, list what you wanted or expected or hoped for from each and, if it all went right or wrong, where. Look at your money habits. Do you spend it as fast as you get it? Do you hoard it 'in case'? Is there never enough? And so on. Take lots of time on this. This doesn't say, by the way, that each repeat of an experience necessarily occurs at exactly the same time. What we need to look for is the repeat of patterns – such as the point in a new relationship where we realize we've done it again! These are the markers, the pointers to unfinished experiences, unlearned lessons.

Exercise 2

This exercise takes place over a long period of time. Find a favourite tree. Sit with your back to the tree, close your eyes, and allow yourself to 'melt into' the tree – as if the two of you are one. Eventually, you will become aware of the life force of the tree. It will be a distinct sensation. The spring or summer is the best time to start this exercise, when the life force is at its strongest. Take a tape recorder with you, or a notebook to record your experiences for comparison with later experiences. Then, revisit the same tree and repeat the process at the turning of each season – just when the leaves are turning in the autumn, when they are budding in the spring, when the tree is barren in the winter, when the tree is in the fulness of life in the summer. The comparisons will be quite profound.

Chapter 7
Out of the fire: the hero's journey

It is often said that a man is his own worst enemy. Certainly the side of ourselves that we must confront when we make the choice for personal growth is the most formidable – that is why it is hidden away deep inside us. There are real risks to be taken – truly, there is no way for you to fully anticipate who you might become through the awakening process. You can discover it only by becoming it.

It is said that 'one swallow doesn't make a summer' – nor does one experience make an inner opening. The opening processes, whatever they may be, will have to be repeated time and time again, but each time the heart becomes a little softer, a little more open to openness. To open our hearts and confront and re-confront ourselves takes courage. It takes a heroic approach to life. It is the quest to discover yourself.

In Egyptian wisdom we find an archetypal model for the human quest in the Isis–Osiris story, where Isis leaves her home and travels far to seek the place where her beloved rests. During her quest, in the palace of the foreign king, she undergoes a transformation within herself – she humbles herself to become a mortal servant – in order to achieve a higher goal. At the end of her quest, out of death – the dead body of Osiris – new life springs: the infant Horus, the falcon, soaring on wings on high.

A modern song encourages us to 'look for the hero inside ourselves'. It is more than just a stirring lyric. It is an essential truism of human development. The basic pattern of life reflects the hero's journey: a child is compelled to give up its childhood and become and adult – to die, you might say, in its infantile personality and psyche and come back as a responsible adult. This is the fundamental transformation that everyone has to undergo: to evolve out of this position of psychological immaturity to the courage of self-responsibility and assurance. Death and resurrection is the basic pattern of the universal hero's journey – leaving one condition and finding the source of life to bring you forth into a richer or mature condition.

There is a universal formula of the mythological hero journey, which Joseph Campbell calls:
1 separation   **2** initiation   **3** return.

The hero ventures forth from the world of common day into a region of supernatural wonder: fabulous forces are there encountered and a decisive victory is won. The hero comes back from this mysterious adventure with the power to bestow boons on his fellow men.

The ultimate aim of the quest must not be solely for oneself, but the wisdom and the power to serve others. When the quest leads to the real inner truth, it is one of the things that truth automatically requires us to do. One of the many distinctions between the celebrity and the hero, is that one lives only for self while the other acts to redeem society.[1] One of the most important ways a hero does this is through his or her own development as a mature, responsible adult. As such, we serve society through the very virtue of our being.

The story of human growth is an archetypal adventure – the story of a child becoming a youth, or the awakening to the new world that opens at adolescence. The rituals of initiation ceremonies in primitive tribes, and most likely in ancient Egypt, are all mythologically grounded and have to do with killing the infantile ego and bringing forth an adult, whether it's the girl or

---

[1] Campbell and Moyers, xv.

the boy. Ceremonies have traditionally given more emphasis to male than female initiation, however. It's harder for the boy to become a man than for the girl to become a woman, because life overtakes the girl and transforms her into a woman whether she wants to or not. But the boy has to make a real effort to be a man. At the first menstruation, the girl becomes a woman. Before she knows it she's pregnant and she transforms into a mother. The boy has to separate himself from his mother, then learn how to be a man, and finally go out into the world to prove himself.

For a boy or a girl, in the beginning you are an obedient dependent, expecting and receiving punishments and rewards. The only way out of this position of psychological immaturity and into the courage of self-responsibility and assurance requires a death and a resurrection. That's the basic pattern of the universal hero's journey – leaving one state of being and finding the source of life to bring you forth into a richer, more mature state of being.

Nor are heroes all men. Men often have a more conspicuous role, just because of the conditions of life. The man has tended to be out in the world and the woman has tended to be in the home. But the Aztecs had a number of heavens to which people's souls were assigned according to the conditions of their death. The heaven for warriors killed in battle was the same for mothers who died in childbirth. Giving birth is definitely a heroic deed, in that it is the giving over of oneself to the life of another. It's a journey – you have to move out of the known, conventional safety of your life to undertake this. You have to be transformed from a maiden to a mother. That's a big change involving many dangers. And when you come back from your journey, with the child, you've brought something for the world. Not only that, you've got a job for life ahead of you.

An essential part of the hero's journey are the trials, tests and ordeals the hero encounters. It is useful to remind ourselves that life is a school and that, as in any school, the most important lessons are often the hardest. The tests of the hero are designed to see to it that the intending hero should really *be* a hero. Is he really a match for his task? Does he have the courage, the knowledge, the capacity, to enable him to serve? Bill Moyers notes:

> In this culture of easy religion, cheaply achieved, it seems to me we've forgotten that all three of the great religions teach that the trials of the hero journey are a significant part of life, that there's no reward without renunciation, without paying the price.[2]

The Koran says, 'Do you think that you shall enter the Garden of Bliss without such trials as came to those who passed before you?' In the gospel of Matthew, Jesus said 'Great is the gate and narrow is the way which leadeth to life, and few there be who find it'.

In our 'fast-everything' culture, many of us have been led to believe that by following the right guru, by joining the right group, by chanting the right mantra, by getting the right crystal, that we will somehow achieve effortless enlightenment. Then we are disappointed and disillusioned when we fail to find satisfaction. Is it really a mystery why?

Isis showed the wisdom of her heroism in her gentle approach to the recovery of Osiris' body. She could have just gone straight to the king and demanded his return. But she understood that a sacrifice of herself was required to demonstrate her worthiness to the king. What the story also implies is that although she might have been a goddess in Egypt, outside of Egypt she was just another ordinary person. As with Isis, when you realize that the real problem is losing yourself, giving yourself to some higher end, or to another – you realize that this itself is the ultimate trial. When we quit thinking primarily about ourselves and our own self-preservation, we undergo a truly heroic transformation of consciousness. Consciousness is transformed either by the trials themselves or by illuminating revelations. The trials and revelations are the real goals of the Quest. The Quest is a cycle, a going and a returning.

The more we surrender, the more we give in to that which we really are, the more we move into paradox. If it isn't paradoxical, it probably isn't divine. The more we surrender

---

[2] Campbell and Moyers.

ourselves, the more we find ourselves. And as we expand our Self-awareness, new worlds open and new dimensions of old worlds unfold. The world becomes a more complex place than we could have imagined. And yet paradoxically, as complexity unfolds, the truth behind it becomes simpler and simpler, until we at last comprehend that All is One.

The hero's journey is modelled for us by our spiritual 'heroes'. Moses ascends the mountain, he meets with Yahweh on the summit of the mountain, and he comes back with rules for the formation of a whole new society. That's the archtypical hero act – departure, fulfilment, return. The Buddha follows a path very much like that of Christ; only 500 years earlier. There is an exact parallel between both saviour figures right down the line, even to the roles and characters of their disciples or apostles; for example, Ananda and St Peter.

Our own development, whether we call it self-actualization, personal growth, psychological development, spiritual awakening, comes to exactly the same thing in the end: to become that which we emulate. Abraham Maslow studied a large number of self-actualized people and he saw parallels between the actual characteristics of the self-actualized and the ideals urged by religion: the transcendence of the ego self; the fusion of the good, the true and the beautiful; wisdom, honesty and naturalness; the transcendence of selfish and personal motivations; increased friendliness and kindness; the easy differentiation between ends (like tranquillity and peace) and means (money, power, status); the decrease of hostility, cruelty, destructiveness, etc. And an increase in decisiveness, self-affirmation and justified anger and indignation.[3]

So, residing deep within each of us is our eternal dimension, often referred to as the soul, the inner being, the higher self, or just the 'Self', the term used in this text.

The Self is described as:
> ...*the most elementary and distinctive part of our being – in other words, its core. This core is of an entirely different nature from all the elements (physical sensations, feelings, thoughts, and so on) that make up our personality. As a*

consequence, it can act as a unifying centre, directing those elements, and bringing them into the unity of an organic wholeness...[4]

At the heart of the Self there is both an active and a passive element, an agent and a spectator. In this sense the Self is not a dynamic in itself; it is a point of witness, a spectator, an observer who watches the flow. But there is another part of the Self – the will-er, or the directing agent – that actively intervenes to orchestrate the various functions and energies of the personality, to make commitments and to instigate action in the external world.[5]

The Self is therefore seen as an integrating centre which *is* the essential person, underlying behaviours, feelings, roles, thoughts, physical manifestations and even gender.

But the Self is also the point of ultimate Oneness with the source of all being – the life of the universe, its stars, planets, atoms, molecules, energies, thoughts, feelings and all else. It is the ultimate goal of all hero journeys and it is only by taking the path of the hero that it can be found.

And where do we find this Self, our own Being of being? In our own hearts. The Egyptians knew this and, at the end of one's life came the symbolic assessment, and the last steps of the hero's journey: The Weighing of the Heart.

Visualization

Finding the hero inside yourself

The first heroic act is the willingness to undertake the process of personal growth, to be willing to take down the barriers between who you have become and who you really are. Truly, there is no way for you to fully anticipate who you might become through the awakening process. You discover it only by becoming it. There are many clues along the way, however, so it is not a totally blind process. The exercises in the earlier

---

[3] Maslow, 1968, p.158.
[4] Brown, p.11.
[5] Brown, p.13.

portion of this book are designed to do just that: to give you a glimmer of who you might be as a fully realized human being, and to start moving you along your pathway.

In this exercise, you will meet a wise Being; it is important to remember that the person you are meeting is yourself. This is not some disincarnate entity, not a spirit guide, not a person outside yourself. It is, in a sense, a projection of the formless Being at the deepest level of your own heart, but that Being projected into human form. It is the person that you have the potential to become, a person in full manifestation of his or her own Humanity.

1 To begin, close your eyes and find yourself back at the head of the avenue of sphinxes, leading to your pyramid. You are dressed in initiation robes and are accompanied by the High Priest or Priestess.

2 At the sound of a gong at the exact moment of sunrise, the moment has come to start your journey.

3 As you reach the ramp leading up into the pyramid, the High Priest or Priestess offers his/her blessing and you proceed alone. The corridor into the centre of the pyramid is lit with torches and, as you walk further inwards, you reach the doorway to the inner chamber and enter.

4 The chamber is lit by a single candle and there is a gold-gilt chair against the right-hand wall of the chamber, where you sit.

5 When you are ready, a shimmering light will gradually appear along the wall opposite you. As the light brightens, a human form will appear within it. Dressed as an Egyptian warrior, or in some other appropriate costume, this figure embodies the deepest strengths within you – the hero within. Strength radiates from this figure, a tangible strength you can feel. Know that this strength is yours and you can draw on it any time you wish. You can converse with this figure and can receive guidance and direction from it.

6 When you feel complete with the experience, the figure will fade. Arise from your chair and return to the entrance to the pyramid, to the bright sunshine. Take a few deep breaths and become aware of your surroundings again. When you are ready, your eyes will open naturally.

Chapter 8
The return of the Goddess

The highest wisdom of the ancient Egyptians was their connection to the flow of life through their oneness with nature, the Goddess Principle. The return of Goddess-consciousness into Western thought holds out the best hope for the continued survival of Westerners. If this seems a dramatic statement, it is intended to be. Look around. Westerners, through their failure to understand their oneness with all life, have been the planetary leaders in the destruction of the environment, the spread of pollution, the annihilation of native people and in promoting self-serving values and beliefs that denigrate nature and separate one person from another. If the wisdom of ancient Egypt teaches us nothing else, it teaches us the sheer idiocy of all this.

Your life, my life, all lives, are part of the great interweaving pattern that is Life. Life is everywhere. Life is all things. Life is never separate from itself. There is no death; there is only Life in its multitude of forms. There is only One.

Western societies in general fail to recognize this; we rear our children as if the exact opposite were true. Psychologists and psychiatrists make profitable careers out of the consequences of this belief.

The ability to perceive the patterns and rhythms of life gives us a choice that no other creature of the earth has. We can choose to live our natural rhythms or to ignore them. When we live them there is a natural sense of pleasure and rightness. When we ignore them we experience dis-ease, ranging from a mild sense of discomfort, a sense that something is missing, to catastrophic physical and mental illness. The tragedy is how few of us even know they exist. When we realize that our own lives are moving, or attempting to move, in a well-regulated, life-sustaining set of rhythms and cycles, we can use them rather than oppose them. It is, in the most profound sense, the return of the Goddess.

How we are separated from Goddess beliefs

In an earlier chapter, we looked at several kinds of mythologies and discovered that in today's Western world we embrace a socially orientated mythology. In it, nature is seen as a thing to be controlled – it is essentially humanity's enemy to be subdued. Nature mythologies and religions are not attempts to control nature but to help you put yourself in accord with it. But when nature is thought of as separate from one's self, and essentially an enemy to be defeated, we don't put ourselves in accord with it. We control it, or try to. The principal means by which we attempt this is through science.

Science

The role of science in our society needs critical re-examination, because in the West science has started to take on a position not unlike that of religion: its products are no longer subject to the verification of the ordinary senses; its language (often mathematics) is spoken by a relative few 'initiates'; its 'truths' must be taken on faith by the vast majority, in that few have the methods or means to test its reality. Paradoxically, that which has given us deeper insight into nature than ever before has also helped to separate us from it. Science has conditioned us not to see the world as it is, but as science sees it. The most damning accusation against an idea or understanding is that it's 'not scientific'. Few understand that science deals in verifiable fragments dealt with by specialists and nowhere is there an overall, integrating overview. Science answers questions of description regarding the forms with which it deals. Nowhere does it deal with that which underlies the forms. Indeed, such questions are deliberately and carefully exorcised from the domain of science.

The base assumption of science seems to be that the future is always better, and it is the role of science to make it that way. What few see is that each advance creates a new set of problems. What even fewer see, is that perhaps science does *not* make a better future. We need only to look at the examples of pesticides, thalidomide and nuclear power, to see that what, at first, appeared to be a boon for humankind has given us an equal menace.

The basic idea of science was revolutionary when it was developed: an objective way of looking at reality that did not depend on beliefs or nationality. The medieval world of religious dogma and hateful superstition, teetering on the brink of collapse as an outmoded system anyway, fell before science. As time went by, science became more and more effective. It produced machines, cured diseases and became an efficient generator of wealth. Because it was so incredibly good at all of this, *few noticed what was being lost along the way*.

Michael Crichton, author of *Jurassic Park*, makes some important observations about science: 'Largely through science, billions of us live on one small world... but science cannot help us decide what to do with that world, or how to live. Science can make a nuclear reactor, *but it cannot tell us not to build it*. Science can make a pesticide, *but it cannot tell us not to use it*.[1]

This underlines one of the most significant criticisms of science: nowhere in it is a human factor. There is, in fact, exactly the opposite – a determined effort to keep it *out*. If human consciousness, and thus human values, are kept out of science, then in science all things are equal. But all things are *not* equal. They either sustain life or they do not. They either fulfil the basic needs of the planet and all life upon it or they do not. If they don't, they are anti-life and are, in the most profound sense, good or bad. The exclusion of humanity from the scientific equation creates a confusing lack of real values in a science-centred society.

[1] Crichton, p.312.

Science has always had a fundamental flaw, aside from being valueless: it asks the questions it can answer and dismisses all other questions as not worth asking. This is underlined in the tendency of science to totally ignore questions of our own humanity, of the human beingness that is the domain of human instinctual life. These are the types of questions science deems not worth asking because it does not have any answers for them.

We can see in the everyday world around us the force for change that humans exert. Today, that force is largely exerted through the products of science, expressed as technology. We are reshaping the world. But that reshaping inevitably takes the forms generated by our own world view. If that world view is distorted, separated from the natural order, then that which we shape must be likewise. Humans are a highly evolved and superbly adapted species, as long as we live in harmony with the world that shapes our evolution. There is an unchanging truth in Nature. Within that truth is the inbuilt interdependence of all creation, both on and beyond the Earth. God is expressed as nature. God *is* nature. Nature is a fundamental truth in and of itself, with or without humans. To challenge that truth with our own limited version of it is the supreme arrogance.

Re-establishing the Goddess principle

And yet, paradoxically, the few truly great scientists have seen beyond the limited tools and abilities of science to discern truth, and discovered a greater world beyond. Physicist Niels Bohr, discoverer of the electron, tells us:

> *For a parallel to the lessons of atomic theory… [we must look to] those kinds of epistemological problems with which already thinkers like the Buddha and Lao Tzu have been confronted, when trying to harmonise our position as spectators and actors in the great drama of existence.*[2]

Physicist Werner Heisenberg states:

> *…one has now divided the world not into different groups of objects but into different groups of connections (inter-relationships)… The world thus appears as a complicated*

---

[2] Bohr, 1958.

tissue of events, in which connections of different kinds alternate or overlap or combine and thereby determine the texture of the whole.[3]

It is a perfect statement in physics of the Goddess principle.

And herein lies the great missed opportunity of science – to use its tools through the guidance of human instinct. There is a golden opportunity to see life and our place in the universe not in bleak, humanless terms, but to see the riches of life which abound in all things. A richness that is invisible to the science that selectively sees only what it can measure, asks itself only the questions it can answer. This is not to condemn science out of hand, but rather is a plea to get science into perspective. Getting the right perspective, understanding the Ma'at of the modern world, is an important step in re-establishing the Goddess principle that the ancient Egyptians understood so well.

One positive role that science can provide, and, indeed, is already starting to provide, is to help us understand our role as creatures of nature. To help us understand that to see ourselves as 'human animals' doesn't demean or degrade us. We need only to watch a few documentaries about other animals to see that they share many human attributes of lovingness, caringness, intelligence and family solidarity. It is the idea that humans are separate from and 'better' than other animals that degrades us with its pettiness. The ancient Egyptians would have been shocked and surprised at such a belief. It is a medieval idea that is still with us, and it is time to let it go too, like the other medieval superstitions that shackled the human spirit for so many centuries.

Human social living

The ancient Egyptians fully understood, if not in sociological terms, at least in practical, everyday-living terms, that the human in-built drive to live and work together is the single most important factor in human survival.

Humans are highly social animals. Our evolutionary success, our every survival as a species, has been dependent on and a

---
[3] Heisenberg, 1958.

direct result of our co-operative nature. Belief systems that set one person against another are a direct threat to our very survival. As it is with other animals that develop patterns of social behaviour, human culture in its variety is an adaptive tool of human evolution specifically evolved to promote the survival of the human species. Each human society develops its own behaviour patterns to suit the unique ecological niche it fills. When we begin to see these differences as a source of richness rather than as a cause for separation, we will make a great leap forward in returning the Goddess.

But:

> *Many modern societies are now fast approaching their limits in terms of size and the impersonality which that size creates. Increasingly we witness violent reactions in massive urban developments to the alienation experienced by their inhabitants... Racism, anti-Semitism and other victimisation of other 'out groups' occur when a sense of frustration is fuelled by feelings of anonymity and detachment. For some members of the 20th-century cultures, the only way of fully understanding themselves is to establish who they are against.*[4]

As we begin to rediscover our essential oneness with and as creatures of nature, we can then allow ourselves to rediscover the needs of the human animal that our 'modern' world often denys us. We can rediscover the natural part of ourselves, the part which governed the everyday lives of the ancient Egyptians.

Social anthropologist Jean Liedloff, who made a landmark study of socially healthy people, concluded that a social system is most desirable which not only takes into account the innate, 'animal' needs, but actually evolves from them. When those needs are fulfilled, there is an inner satisfaction, a fulfilment that can never be achieved from rampant consumerism. The result is less demand on the environment and a healthier society in all respects.

The expectation of the newly born member of the human species is that he/she will be born into a suitable culture, i.e. one

---

[4] Morris and Marsh, pp.21–2.

which will supply him/her with innate needs. There is nothing in his/her evolutionary past to prepare him/her for a society that doesn't. The person expects to be born into a culture that will support a life-long quest for self-development. And the person expects that his/her culture will have, as a consequence, a supporting, inbuilt natural stability, as opposed to the, illusory, artificially imposed stability of modern societies that will limit him/her, denying his/her birthright of lifelong growth. It is one of the most important lessons we can learn from ancient Egyptian society: when these principles are followed, the society lasts – 3,000 years, no less. And, when they are abandoned as they were in the last centuries BC in Egypt, the society declines and collapses.

Re-examining our beliefs

Moving back towards nature will bring forth the mother principle again. The mother loves all her children – 'the stupid ones, the bright ones, the naughty ones, the good ones'. Hence the difficulty in God-the-Father religions of including 'out groups', i.e. those who do not belong to that particular religion or subscribe to a differing set of beliefs. It doesn't matter what their particular character is. The feminine represents the inclusive love for progeny – the progeny of all life.

As we re-examine the role of science, so too must we re-examine the role of religion. Campbell states correctly that religion is really a kind of second womb. It is designed to bring this extremely complicated thing, which is a human being, to maturity, which means to be self-motivating, self-acting.

Much of Western religion deals with only the 'spiritual' side of life, as if it is separate from all the rest of life.

In an interview in 1987, journalist Bill Moyers asked Joseph Campbell:

> *Don't you think modern Americans have rejected the ancient idea of nature as a divinity because it would have kept us from achieving dominance over nature? How can you cut down trees and uproot the land and turn the rivers into real-estate without killing God?*

To which Campbell replied:
> *Yes, but that's not simply a characteristic of modern Americans, that is the biblical condemnation of nature which they inherited from their own religion and brought with them, mainly from England. God is separate from nature, and nature is condemned of God. It's right there in Genesis: we are to be masters of the world.*

He continued:
> *But if you will think of ourselves as coming out of the earth, rather than having been thrown in here from somewhere else, you see that we are the earth, we are the consciousness of the earth. These are the eyes of the earth. And this is the voice of the earth.*

The necessity for a return to nature has been emphasized again and again. It may appear that there have been relatively few practical suggestions, a '12-point plan' for 'returning'. But the problem is not so much in what we *do*, but rather in how we *think*.

The environment

Management of the environment has, from the beginnings of agriculture, come increasingly within human domain. Humans evolved as hunter-gatherers, and environmental management has never been part of our evolutionary background. If there was fruit to be found, humans ate. If there was game to be hunted, humans ate. If not, we went hungry. We are not instinctive environmental managers – it is a learned skill. The Egyptian management of the Nile as an effective renewer of the soil and regenerator of life is a model example. When guided by instinctive values, that skill can be exercized effectively; but that is the point: it is a skill; not an instinct. There is ample archaeological evidence that time and time again, villages, towns and cities have had to be abandoned because of resource exhaustion. A few hours of television news are convincing evidence that as a species, we haven't learned much since then.

Because humans are not instinctive environmental managers it doesn't mean that we are not instinctively in touch with our environment. The flood of people from the cities into the countryside each weekend is evidence enough of this. Yet how much distance we have from 'natural man' is measured in the relative insensitivity of the most ardent city escapee compared with the sensitivity exhibited by 'native' peoples who still live close to the earth. It is this insensitivity that permits us to perpetrate outrages against nature on a monumental scale.

The Goddess and individuality

We also need to re-examine the over-emphasis on individuality in the West. We are bound up in the illusion that we are totally independent of others. The Egyptians would have been astonished at such a thought.

Ashley Montagu calls this illusion the 'myth of the individual' and emphasizes its dangers to society. Every person through childhood training, is irrevocably bound to the group in which they have been socialized. All of us, even psychopaths, have *some* connection to others. Unless we live alone on desert islands, to some degree at least, some of our needs are met by others. The principal danger that Montagu sees in the creation of separateness where separateness does not exist through 'individuality', is that it 'neglects to teach the moral obligation of independent thought, the responsibility to challenge unsound ideas and conventions, the right to protest, and the bounden duty to object'. It is the basis of an 'anything goes' society. As a result of this illusion, the values of society are focused solely around 'the individual', which promotes narcissistic introspection, self-absorption and self-consciousness.

Loosening the family tie

Finally, and perhaps most important of all, is another area of modern life that the ancient Egyptians would have looked upon with foreboding: the loosening of family ties and the virtual abandonment of traditional family life. From what we know of Egyptian life, although the actual rituals of marriage are unknown, there is ample evidence that family life was the very bedrock of Egyptian civilization. We do not need to return to the totalitarian patriarchal family, but return to the family we must. There can be *no* return to the full wisdom of ancient Egypt without the reinstatement of the family as the centre of our lives.

Marriage is a public statement of commitments and this, in turn, builds other commitments. It is important for social involvement, personal security, for creating role models and providing the moral capital of the next generation. Patricia Morgan of the Institute of Economic Affairs, and author of *Farewell to the Family*, rightly points out that membership of a family gives individuals a stake in the future, the men a role in life and a place in the community, and children a stable start with two parents for whom their offspring's welfare is their paramount and joint concern. Without marriage and the family, we lose our links to the rest of the community, our sources of support in adversity and care in old age. These amount to the loss of the framework of society itself. In Liedloff's studies of social health, family bonding was identified as the *key* element in social stability.

Meditation

Perhaps the greatest wisdom of the ancient Egyptians is that life itself is a meditation – a constant living, moving experience of life in its many forms. Because the ancient Egyptians did not separate themselves from the whole of life, they would have never thought in such terms. It is only because we in the 'modern' world have done so that we need to think thusly. But think it we must, if we are to re-establish the vital links to the life force that sustains us all.

And so, the final exercise. As you go through your daily life, pause at every opportunity to reach out and connect with all that is around you. As you do so, you will quickly find that some connections bring a feeling of pleasure and enrichment. Others will feel disturbing and profoundly un-natural. Feed life to those which uplift you; withdraw life from those which do not. You will know the difference.

REFERENCES

★These titles are recommended reading

★*Ancient Egyptian Book of the Dead* Trans. R.O. Faulkner, British Museum Publications, 1979

★*Ancient Egyptian Pyramid Texts* Trans. R.O. Faulkner, Oxford: Oxford University Press, 1969

★Appleyard, Brian *Understanding the Present: Science and the Soul of Modern Man* Picador (London) 1992

Beckman, Robert *Downwave*, London: Pan, 1983

Bohr, Neils *Atomic Physics and Human Knowledge*, New York: John Wiley & Sons, 1958

★Brown, Molly Young *The Unfolding Self*, Los Angeles: Psychosynthesis Press, 1983

Bunning, Erwin *The Physiological Clock*, Berlin and New York: Springer-Verlag, 1973

★Campbell, Joseph *Myths to Live By*, London: Bantam, 1972

★Campbell, Joseph and Moyers, Bill *The Power of Myth*, London: Doubleday, 1988

Crichton, Michael *Jurassic Park*, New York: Ballantine, 1990

★Emery, W.B. *Archaic Egypt*, London: Penguin, 1987

Encyclopedia Britannica

Encyclopedia of Mythology, London: Mandarin, 1975

Etkin, William 'Behavioural Factors Stabilizing Social Organizations in Humans', in Zubin and Hunt, 1965

Gauquelin, Michel *Astrology and Science*, London: Peter Davies, 1969

Gauquelin, Michel *The Cosmic Clocks* London: Peter Owen, 1967

★Grimal, Nicolas *A History of Ancient Egypt*, Cambridge: Blackwell, 1992

Hancock, Graham *Fingerprints of the Gods*, London: Mandarin, 1995

Harrison, John M.D. *Love Your Disease*, London: Angus and Robertson, 1984

Healy, D. and Williams, J.M.H. 'Disrhythmia, Dysphoria, and Depression: The Interaction of Learned Helplessness and Circadian Disrhythmia in the Pathogenesis of Depression', *Psychological Bulletin*, 1988, Vol. 103, No. 2, 163–78

Heisenberg, W. *Physics and Philosophy*, New York: Harper Torchbooks, 1958

★Liedloff, Jean *The Continuum Concept*, London: Penguin, 1986

Lowen, Alexander *Bioenergetics*, London: Penguin: 1975

Lowen, Alexander, *Pleasure*

Lunar Effect, Hastings House (New York), 1996

Montagu, Ashley *Growing Young*, Granby: Bergin and Garvey, 1989

★Maslow, Abraham, *Toward a Psychology of Being*, New York: Van Norstrand-Reinhold, 1968

Morgan, Patricia 'Family Crisis Affects Us All', The (London) *Daily Express*, 29 Aug, 1996

Morris, Desmond *The Naked Ape*, London: Corgi, 1967

Morris, Desmond and Marsh, Peter *Tribes*, Salt Lake City, Peregrine, 1988

Moss, Richard M.D. *The I That is We*, Berkeley: Celestial Arts, 1981

Palmer, John D. *An Introduction to Biological Rhythms*, New York: Academic Press, 1976

★Rodegast, Pat and Stanton, Judith *Emmanual's Book*, New York: Bantam, 1985

Rosenzweig, Mark and Leiman, Arnold *Physiological Psycholgy*, New York: Random House, 1989

★Speake, Graham Ed. *Atlas of Ancient Egypt*, Oxford: Equinox, 1980

The Papyrus Ebers, Trans. B. Ebbell, London: Oxford University Press, 1937

Whitman, John *The Psychic Power of Plants*, London: Star Books, 1973, 134

Zubin, Joseph and Hunt, Howard *Comparative Psychopathology, Animal and Human*, New York: Grune and Stratton, 1967

Zurbrugg, Rolf P. 'Hypothalamic-Pituitary-Adrenocortical Regulation', in *Monographs in Paediatrics*, London: S. Karger, 1976